PRAISE FOR IT

"Many of our challenges are rc
Does your worthiness come from within you o
It's Within You Rabbi Aryeh Weinstein and Dr. Ilene S. Cohen present a clear and comprehensive approach on how to live your life inside out instead of outside in. A superb contribution, with the power to enhance and transform the lives of its readers."

– **Simon Jacobson**, Author of *Toward a Meaningful Life*

"In a world lacking confidence in personal life skills and a deficient moral compass, the authors have compiled a wisdom-laden, and confidently prescriptive manual that provides direction and content to our lives, skillfully embracing spiritual authenticity and professional experience. Highly recommended reading."

– **Rabbi Dr. Laibl Wolf**, Author of best-selling *Practical Kabbalah* and Internationally-acclaimed Lecturer

"When I saw that, *It's Within You* was co-written by a Rabbi, I assumed it would be too religious for my taste, but I was pleasantly surprised to be completely wrong! I consider myself to be a relatively confident person and wasn't expecting to read anything that I didn't already know but the humble yet provoking nature of this book not only opened my eyes to new perspectives but challenged me to dig even deeper and fine tune my "worthiness" muscle. It's encouraged me to see the areas of my life where I feel frustrated and fed up with others, and taught me tools to change my approach. I'll be using some of these stories and strategies with my own clients!"

– **Jasmin Terrany, LMHC**, Psychotherapist, Author & Speaker, www.JasminTerrany.com

"*It's Within You* will allow any person who values self-discovery and growth, to take an in-depth look into the power of their own influence on their life. Along with the end of chapter activities, this book allows you to put into practice the concepts that you read. I would definitely recommend this book to my clients, family, and friends. Kudos authors!"

– EDRICA D. RICHARDSON, PHD., Licensed Marriage and Family Therapist, www.dredrich.com

"*It's Within You* is the intersection of psychotherapy, religion, and spirituality that examines the concept of self-worth and how people can enhance their "solid self" in a world where we all wear masks. Asking simple but profound questions, using both their personal and professional experiences, the authors guide readers to a deeper understanding of self and others. The book offers a challenge for the reader to consider: Do you have the courage to look inward and change? It reads like a meditation on intentional living. I recommend it to anyone who wants to be more at home in their life."

– JIM RUDES, PH.D., LMFT, LCSW
Associate Professor, Barry University

"By providing practical examples and activities based off ancient wisdom, Dr. Ilene and Rabbi Weinstein open up a whole new window into the source of true happiness. *It's Within You,* is a transformative guide that has helped me find my own inner-worthiness and create happiness from within myself! The tools provided in this book are necessary for anyone looking to make real change in their life. Highly recommend."

– CORINNE DEBACHER, Journalism Teacher
at Nova HighSchool

"I loved it, connected with it, and believe, *It's Within You,* is very impactful and meaningful. I love the way Judaism is woven into the book in a way that makes it feel spiritual and not religious, the way real-life examples helped you connect more with the purpose of the book, and the exercises and "nuggets" that closed the chapters. Happy to have spent my weekend with this masterpiece!"

— MICHELLE DEMPSEY, Author of *Very Well-Written*

"No matter who you are or what you're living through, *It's Within You* has something valuable to offer. With their fresh perspective on timeless wisdom, Cohen and Weinstein have created an informal guide to daily living as practical as it is profound."

— DR. DENISE FOURNIER, Evergreen Therapy

"An informative guide for those who want to be accountable and create self-driven change in their lives and relationships. *It's Within You* offers helpful illustrations, exercises, and metaphors to stimulate critical thinking, in order to be less reactive and more mature in all relationships."

— OLIVIA SCHLAPFER COLMER, PH.D., LMFT

It's Within You

A Detailed Road Map to Igniting Deeper Self-Worth, Richer Relationships and Greater Personal Freedom

RABBI ARYEH WEINSTEIN

ILENE S.COHEN, Ph.D.

A POWERFUL SYNTHESIS OF MODERN
PSYCHOLOGY AND ANCIENT SPIRITUAL WISDOM

HARTE & CO PUBLISHING • MIAMI FLORIDA

It's Within You:
A Detailed Road Map to Igniting Deeper Self-Worth
Richer Relationships and Greater Personal Freedom

by Rabbi Aryeh Weinstein and Ilene S. Cohen, Ph.D.

Published by Harte & Co Publishing, Miami FL

Editor: Denise Fournier
Book design: Book Savvy Studio

Library of Congress Control Number: 2019903122
ISBN: 978-0-9993115-1-6
First Edition
Printed in the United States of America

DEDICATION

To my wife, Rosie, whose unconditional acceptance
has revealed so much I never knew was there.
To my children, Uziel, Raizel, Esther, Hinda, Nachman,
Chana, Menucha Rochel, Menachem Mendel, and Shayna.
My eyes wash over with tears of joy when I think of you.
Please know that wherever you may be, I am with you.

— Rabbi Aryeh Weinstein

To my amazing, tenacious, and loving daughters, Emily and
Elizabeth, I hope that through my unconditional love, you will
always see yourselves as I see you. Please never doubt your
worth, and know that you are forever loved.

— Ilene S. Cohen

CONTENTS

Birth is G-d saying you matter.

– SIMON JACOBSON

PREFACE

When the soul is starved for nourishment, it lets us know with feelings of emptiness, anxiety, or yearning.

— THE REBBE

"YOU'VE GOT TO GET YOUR LIFE TOGETHER!" How many times have you heard these words, or said them to yourself when feeling frustrated? Maybe it was said to you, or maybe you've yelled it to someone you love. Perhaps your parents said it to you in a moment of anger. Or maybe, in your anxiety about one of your own children's inability to launch into adulthood, you've said it or thought it on what feels like a million occasions.

It's possible you bought this book with the intention of giving it to someone who should probably get their act together. If that's the case, we're sure you're coming from a place of real caring; the problem, however, is that when we're so focused on others, we can end up with a major blind spot that doesn't let us see the changes we need to make within ourselves. Most of us think that if only the people in our lives would change, we'd be able to move happily forward with our lives. It's easier to think that if we can get people to change—or avoid certain difficult people altogether—we'll be free to have the problem-free life we envision for ourselves.

We've found that this path of pushing others to change doesn't deliver long-lasting happiness or fulfillment. If every time we encounter a new drama in our relationships, we blame others or try to change them, we'll end up pretty disappointed.

We might become resentful when we try to help others and they don't improve or, instead, we might cut the people who disappoint us completely out of our lives. Real change takes place when we learn to observe ourselves in our relationships and appreciate that problems don't come from other people, but rather from the connections between us. Understanding that we play a part in contributing to the problems we face isn't exactly the easiest realization; few of us like to think we could benefit from making changes. However, when we're willing to be honest with ourselves and work on the only part of our relationships and lives that we can actually change, the benefits—for ourselves and others—are endless.

This book addresses a big question: *Are you willing to take a good look at yourself and make changes, instead of insisting that others need to change?* It may sound like a lot of hard work to fold into your already busy life, but it offers an opportunity to make true, meaningful, and lasting changes. Imagine living with control over your emotions, your responses to others, and your life in general—a life that isn't dictated by your circumstances, but instead ruled by how you decide to view and live it.

Stepping Up to the Challenge

We want you to know that we don't take commitment for change lightly. We're fully aware of how difficult it is to recognize that you need to work on yourself; and we know it's even harder to actually make meaningful and productive changes, even when you're aware of the potential they have to benefit you. In our efforts to write and teach the concepts in this book, we've come to understand that the journey of making your own changes is transformative, as long as you commit to the process. We also recognize that this is by no means an easy process. There may be times when you feel that you aren't making significant progress;

please don't let that stop you. Sometimes we have to take a few steps back before we can move forward.

It's also important to keep in mind that this book isn't just a bunch of concepts for you to learn; it's meant to offer a new way of thinking—one that comes from traditional Jewish ideas and a family therapy model known as Bowen Family Systems Theory. However, the book isn't intended for an exclusively Jewish or psychology-minded audience; anyone can apply the ideas contained within it. Our intention is to give grounded and practical advice that anyone can benefit from considering. We occasionally reference G-d, Jewish figures, and psychology research to support our position, as we believe this adds richness and uniqueness to our message. But if you have a different faith or aren't religious at all, you can still greatly benefit from the ideas we're sharing. We merely hope to share with you a way of thinking that can improve your quality of life.

In the different chapters of this book, you'll experience distinct breakthroughs. Each chapter presents new concepts, with plenty of examples and stories to help you understand why this information is important. However, it's good to remember that the transformation you'll experience through this book won't happen while you're reading the lesson; it will happen when you put what you've learned into practice through the activities at the end of each chapter. These are vital. They don't take a lot of time, but they will require some introspection. The more thought you give to these activities, the more you'll get out of them. It's a well-known fact that change begins with action. You'll likely find it most helpful to concentrate on one chapter at a time, applying each activity to your life for as long as you believe you're making meaningful changes.

What's most important is that you be intentional about applying the concepts without feeling constrained by time. Learning new behaviors takes a lot of patience, persistence, and time; there's no need to rush. Our hope is that, after learning the different concepts in this book, you'll see a change in the way you respond to different experiences and people in your life, which will lead you to feel a sense of worth, value, connection, and control over your emotions, so that you see yourself living a life you choose, rather than one you're merely floating through. We're confident that you'll experience significant improvement in your life through this book because we've gone through—and continue to go through—everything we'll be teaching you.

INTRODUCTION

WRITTEN BY ILENE S. COHEN, PH.D.

*The keys to liberation are clenched tightly
in the fists of our own egos.*

— TZVI FREEMAN, *Bringing Heaven Down to Earth*

POP QUIZ! What's the one thing no human on this planet can live without?

If you answered *oxygen*, you're correct. We rely on many things for our survival, and the most basic of them is oxygen. You can survive for a few days without water, food, or shelter, but you can't stay alive for more than a few minutes without oxygen. And it isn't enough to just breathe oxygen; it has to be clean as well. Yes, we can survive on polluted air, but we pay a hefty price for it in the long run. The absence of clean air to breathe shows up as a significant lack in performance, affecting our focus, energy, and sharpness. It also leads to a variety of illnesses.

While oxygen is necessary for the survival of your physical body, your emotional and spiritual wellbeing relies on what I view as another form of oxygen—something that goes beyond basic survival. It's the knowledge that you are worthy, invaluable, and indispensable. This knowledge is the oxygen that sustains your mental wellbeing, allowing you to optimize your quality of life. The clearer you are about your inherent value and purpose, the more effectively you can step into your responsibility and fulfill your purpose. Your individual value and worth can *never* be fulfilled by someone or something else because they're part of YOU; they come from your core self, not from outside influences. They come from G-d putting you here for a purpose. This is what makes you inherently worthy. Can there be anything better than realizing your inherent value and no longer needing to seek it from the world around you? We sure don't think so. For us, that sense of worthiness is priceless.

The less clear we are about our inherent worthiness, the weaker we believe ourselves to be; this affects our determination, resilience, drive, and sense of self. Living with a lack of personal clarity is similar to breathing polluted air. It weakens our performance, affecting our energy and mental clarity. It also creates many forms of emotional pain, discontentment, and loneliness. Sounds pretty detrimental, don't you think? That's why we wrote this book: to help you develop a clear understanding of your worth so that you can start making changes in your life. By taking steps toward change, you can clean your daily intake of oxygen and live in ways that are more congruent with who you're meant to be. Not only can this help you create a meaningful life, it can also help you cultivate peace, joy, and internal calm.

Seeking Worthiness

There are two essential ways we seek out a sense of worthiness, and the particular path we choose has enormous implications for our quality of life. We either seek worthiness from within, or we seek it from without. When we seek worthiness from within and become aware of our inherent value, we become emotionally and spiritually healthy and strong. Basically, we become unstoppable, only relying on our inherent selves to know who we are and what kind of life we're meant to live. We become more focused and attuned to our personal purpose and mission. We ultimately become calm and centered creators of our own destiny, living in a world that's controlled by internal forces rather than external circumstances.

When we seek worthiness from outside ourselves, we depend on the people, things, and circumstances around us to tell us we're worthy. We become dependent on everything and everyone, hoping they'll soothe our internal struggle. We worship people, material objects, and financial success like false gods, hoping they'll provide us with the oxygen we so desperately crave. The great American poet Robert Frost wrote in *The Road Not Taken*, "Two roads diverged in a wood, and I—I took the one less traveled by, and that has made all the difference." Which road will you choose?

The Facts

Just as we must have oxygen to survive, we must also have a sense of worthiness; our emotional and spiritual survival depends on it. And just as the quality of the oxygen we breathe directly affects our physical health, so it is with the quality of our spiritual and emotional oxygen. When our worthiness is based on outside sources, our oxygen source is polluted and we tend to feel unhealthy. Relying on external rewards as motivation keeps us beholden to the people around us. When we can find ways to internally derive our worthiness, we feel better about ourselves and are much less likely to strive for meaningless relationships, stay in jobs we hate, or act in ways that don't reflect who we truly are.

So now that you understand the importance of internal worthiness, what's next? Well, first you must distinguish where you get your sense of worthiness from. Is it from external rewards, or does it come from within? Do you sometimes feel a sense of worthiness by just being yourself, but other times feel like you're not enough when surrounded by certain people? Sometimes it's hard to answer questions like these, and it's impossible to be objective about them. Nobody can introspect when there's so much emotion attached to their ideas of themselves. One easy way to assess where our self-worth comes from is to observe our actions, words, and thoughts. I recommend beginning by taking a close look at your actions. Ask yourself, "Is my life spent reacting or responding to others? Do I spend more time answering to the people around me, or am I more intentional with my responses? When I'm part of a group discussion, do I offer my opinion regardless of the outcome, or do I heavily react to others' opinions?

I once heard a story about a brilliant man. Any time someone would share an opinion with him, he'd argue by giving the opposite viewpoint. They say that when this man died, his soul stood before the A-lmighty, who turned to him and said, "On Earth, you were known to be a brilliant intellect. Why don't you share a brilliant idea with us and show us what you have achieved?" The man responded, "G-d, why don't you share a brilliant idea, and I'll refute it?" This short story demonstrates the tragedy of a person who never owns the very place G-d created for them and instead plays it safe by living in reaction instead of responding to life—living with a sense of self-worth from without instead of beginning within.

Getting Started

The following quiz will provide you with a starting point to measure your sense of worthiness and see whether you tend to seek it from within or without. Remember that each and every one of us has a foundation of intrinsic worthiness to build on; so no matter what, you won't be starting from ground zero.

Maybe you're starting to wonder whether you're a worthy person at all. Maybe you're beginning to think that a lack of internal worth is contributing to—or the reason for—your anxiety, health issues, or inability to maintain successful and satisfying relationships. Or, perhaps, you've determined that you gain your worthiness from external resources, but you don't think it's something you need to change.

No matter where you are in your personal process, this quiz will help you find out whether your lack of worthiness is a major issue in your life so you can start making some important changes. You deserve the freedom to make the best choices for *you*. You deserve to feel worthy. No, you have an *obligation* to feel worthy. After all, you were gifted by G-d with your life and expected to make the best of it! If the quiz reveals that you're seeking worthiness from without, this book will offer you some helpful next steps that will change your life.

The quiz has 22 True or False questions that will allow you to assess the status of your self-worth. Read each statement and consider how much it corresponds with how you feel. Your answers should reflect your personal experience. Don't judge your responses, just answer authentically as you go. Remember, these are True or False questions, so mark a T or F for every response.

___ It's very important for me to be liked by everyone I meet.

___ I feel uncomfortable around successful and confident people.

___ I'm not a very worthwhile person.

___ I find myself doing more for others, even feeling used at times, so that people will like me.

___ I'm not as valuable as anyone else.

___ The need for approval from others comes before how I feel about myself.

___ I don't have many unique qualities.

___ I have more unpleasant feelings about myself than I do pleasant ones.

___ Overall, I feel like a failure.

___ I wish I had someone else's life.

___ Thinking I may have to confront someone makes me feel uneasy, and sometimes I get physically sick over it.

___ It's very difficult for me to express myself.

___ I don't like myself when others reject me.

___ I have to give all of myself in order to receive love.

___ I do a lot to try to make others happy, including ignoring my own needs.

___ I'm very sensitive to others' comments.

___ I should never let people disapprove of my actions.

___ I sometimes feel like love is a transaction, and I'm "buying" my friends by always doing things for them.

___ I'm only as worthy as the amount of money I have in my bank account.

___ I know I do something right when I get praise from others.

___ I do things even if they don't fall in line with my personal values.

___ I always accept the latest trends.

Scoring Your Answers

So, are you getting your worthiness from within or without? And how is this affecting your life? To find out, generate your total score by counting the number of times you marked True for your answer. Then read the section that corresponds with your score.

Between 16 and 22: If your score falls in this range, you're getting your sense of worthiness from without. Living this way significantly affects your ability to live your own life, find your purpose, and have fulfilling relationships. It's time to start making changes in your life so you can finally feel good enough!

Between 10 and 15: If your score falls in this range, your sense of worthiness sometimes comes from within and other times from without, depending on the situation. This is enough to affect your life in a negative way. It's important for you to address this pattern because it could become worse over time.

Between 5 and 9: If you fall in this range, you're probably maintaining some good relationships, and your life hasn't been significantly affected by feeling a lack of internal worthiness. You have the strength and resilience to know you're worthy, regardless of your external circumstances. Keep in mind that scoring in this range reveals you still have some tendencies to seek worthiness outside yourself, which could create some downfalls in your life. Keep building on your internal strength in an effort to bring down your score.

4 or less: If your score is in this range, you have a strong sense of worthiness that comes from within. However, it wouldn't hurt to identify when you do seek approval from the outside so that it doesn't progress. This is a great time to create more self-awareness and learn some new tools that could spare you trouble down the road.

My Personal Experience

Now, before you get down on yourself about your score, I want to share something personal with you. When I took this quiz just a few years ago, my score was close to 22. So believe me when I say that I know how hard it is to never feel good enough, always doubting yourself and your value. Growing up, I discovered that I had a certain way of dealing with life, which I thought helped guide me through some tough times. I reached for external resources to soothe an internal pain. I continued to engage in the same behavior patterns, thinking I would get the outcome I wanted. I thought if only I worked hard enough, made others happy, and bought enough stuff, then I'd finally feel valuable. But the more I reached for my worth by trying to accomplish external goals, the more I saw that it was like trying to hold sand in a cheese grater or reach a destination on a treadmill. Nothing stuck. Nothing I did got me anywhere good. But instead of changing my strategy, I just kept doing more of the same, believing once I had enough success, friends, and money, I'd finally feel worthy. What I didn't realize was that my approach needed to be dismantled. More external rewards weren't the answer; they never were.

I truly believed that by constantly aiming to achieve major accomplishments, I was making everyone—including myself—happy. As time went on, however, I started to realize that this strategy wasn't working very well at all. As my appetite for more became overwhelming, my drive to find what would truly make me happy grew stronger. I had spent my life constantly giving in and doing things for other people, negotiating things that should have been non-negotiable in my relationships. Living without an internal sense of worthiness held me back in many aspects of my life. I wasn't able to say no. I felt guilty all the time. I didn't do things for myself. I strived hard for dreams that weren't even my own. Eventually, I found myself empty, alone, and endlessly exhausted. My relationships became one-sided; they seemed to work fine for everyone else in my life, but they were no longer working for *me*. I started to lose myself in my relationships with others and thought that if only I could do a little bit more, I'd feel better about myself. But this didn't work. In fact, it had the opposite effect.

For years, I tried to find myself by losing myself in my relationships with others, my career, and my endless pursuit of material things. Naturally, it didn't work. I wound up feeling alone and lost, at a complete standstill in my life. Although I knew the way I was living wasn't working, I still had a strong urge to work harder and do more. I thought maybe I just hadn't reached the point of true success and happiness yet. The truth is, my sense of self-worth wasn't very strong. I looked confident and successful on the outside, but on the inside, I was my worst critic. I felt lost and worthless. Accomplishing big goals made me feel euphoric at first; but after the high wore off, I realized I still wasn't satisfied. I never felt complete. I thought, if only I could get better at what I was doing, I would finally feel good enough.

At first, I wrongly thought that if other people in my life would change—if they would only just appreciate me—then I could finally feel worthy. I also used to tell myself that all my troubles would melt away once I found the perfect relationship. What I didn't realize is that I wasn't going to find the type of relationships I wanted unless I started to discover my inherent value, independent of others.

Constantly falling into the trap of never feeling worthy, I eventually started to wonder if accomplishing my big dreams would ever truly make me happy. Would I ever find a way to feel complete and content? Exploring this question marked the first step of my journey. Through my own process of self-discovery, I went from being a person with the self-esteem of a dish rag to someone self-accepting and aware of her worth. More than anything, I want the same for you. Living the way I used to live was like eating five plates of food at a buffet but still wanting more. Never feeling fully satisfied and always seeking external indulgences to feel internally worthy is no way to live

How It All Begin

One of the richest stories in the Bible is that of Adam and Eve, narrated in the book of *Genesis*. By eating from the forbidden fruit of the Tree of Knowledge, Adam and Eve acquire the awareness of good and evil and are then expelled from the Garden of Eden.

Before they ate the forbidden fruit, they were transparent in their relationship with G-d; their egos didn't block their awareness of the purpose of creation. Even those things they did for themselves—as we all must—were not about themselves, but about their purpose. The moment they acted according to their own personal desires rather than their purpose, they became confused by self-consciousness and were no longer transparent. Suddenly, another agenda entered the picture: an absorption with self. This led them to disconnect from their relationship with G-d.

Before they ate fruit from the Tree of Knowledge, Adam and Eve "were both naked, and were not ashamed" (*Genesis*, 2:25). Although they were aware of their own nakedness before they ate the fruit, it didn't cause them shame. This was because their entire being was dedicated to their purpose of creation. Only after they ate the forbidden fruit, after acting purely for self, did they experience a lack of integrity and transparency. Now, they experienced everything through two lenses: an authentic one and a self-oriented one. Bias and self-orientation took away their integrity. They became self-conscious about their bodies, no longer seeing them as transparent tools for a purpose. Now they represented a pursuit of selfish indulgence.

The serpent tells Eve: "When you eat of [the fruit of the Tree of Knowledge] your eyes will be opened" (*Genesis*, 3:5). Of course, Eve's eyes were technically already open. She wasn't physically blind; she was already aware of her nakedness. Her eyes became open to self-consciousness. This awareness of self altered and confused Adam and Eve's very understanding, dissolving the boundaries between themselves and their purpose. Working through this confusion to the best of our ability is what this book explains. We all have a transparent, authentic self, and a self-oriented, indulgent self. When we take a moment to stand outside these two selves and learn to differentiate between them, we can experience liberation.

Have you ever felt, upon learning new information or arriving at a new insight, that you've somehow known it all along? This is a common experience which shows that certain knowledge lies hidden in the cracks of awareness, even though we aren't self-reflectively aware of it. Then, when an event triggers an idea into our awareness, we suddenly become open to the fact that we were conscious of the knowledge all along. This is how it goes when we become aware of our worth. It isn't something we find or seek out; it's something we discover that we had all along.

During the Renaissance, Europeans became aware of the three-dimensional perspective. Some authors refer to this development as the *discovery of perspective.* Well, it obviously wasn't the creation of perspective. Every sight-capable human being has had visual perspective since the dawn of the species. But in this 15th Century discovery, European artists became aware, for the first time, that they were *conscious of* perspective. Three-dimensional perspective wasn't new in consciousness, but in the field of self-awareness. After it entered this field, it was recognized as something people had always known, but hadn't known they'd known.

It's critical for ordinary human thinking that we not only know something, but be aware that we know it as well. There's a difference between knowledge and self-awareness of knowledge or, in other words, knowing that we know something. The way we rectify the fundamental human challenge, the confusion created by the fruit of the Tree of Knowledge, is by learning to *know what* we experience, to become self-aware. It allows us to recognize ourselves through our experiences and to think about our own thoughts, feelings, and sensations.

There's a great deal of good that comes from self-knowledge, awareness, and reflection. It gives us a chance to realize the fullness of human potential and fulfill its role in the scheme of things. The human intellect has the unique ability to *stand outside* its own thoughts, as it's capable of thinking about its own thoughts. We, humans, can also stand outside our emotions by pondering those emotions. We can even stand outside ourselves by contemplating our place in the world as if we were looking at ourselves from the outside. This capacity is what we call self-reflective awareness, and it's for making sense of nature. Without it, we'd be completely immersed in our instincts, unable to understand our actions and sense of worth. Only through self-awareness can we think objectively and consciously live our lives from a place of value. Our capacity for self-awareness is nature's only chance of solving the mystery of life. Think about this for a moment: without our capacity for self-reflection, we would stand no chance of understanding ourselves; we would never be able to rise above our own instinctive reactions.

Great suffering and confusion came to us when we gained a sense of ourselves. This issue is at the core of our success and failure. It determines whether we're self-centered or purpose-oriented. The *confusion exists in the relationship between ourselves and the world around us.* We have a remarkable ability to invest fully in something other than ourselves, knowing that we can be self-reflective while remaining connected to everything around us. The conflict lies in making a choice between living consumed in our awareness of self or totally immersed in our relationships with others.

Successful athletes at their peak performance talk about losing a sense of themselves when they're engrossed in their sport. Can you think of a time when you were so focused on what you were doing that you lost a sense of everything around you? A time when you transcended what you were doing so that nothing else existed outside the present moment? That must have been what living in the Garden was like. Now, the tricky thing is that some of us can get so focused on, and consumed with ourselves that we disconnect completely from the present moment. Part of our dilemma is finding a balance between focusing on ourselves and focusing on our connection to everything else. We don't want to focus so much on ourselves that we lose sight of others, but we don't want to be so focused outside ourselves that we lose a sense of ourselves either. Finding the path to ensuring our focus on ourselves isn't about ourselves but rather about our purpose.

Throughout this book, we'll be posing many questions to you. We've crafted these questions so you can work through the confusion that came to us when we developed a sense of ourselves. Working through this confusion allowed us to become more self-aware and knowledgeable of our worthiness while remaining connected to those around us. We created this book to offer the same opportunity to you.

Our fundamental challenge as humans is to differentiate between objective and subjective reality. When we become aware of ourselves, we develop the natural drive to personalize everything. The success of our happiness develops when we form a strong sense of worth that allows us to go beyond self. Musicians whose fingers play on their own can only master losing their sense of self once they've fully immersed themselves in the hardships of learning a new instrument.

This book is a guide to mastering your sense of self and self-worth so you can connect with others and the world around you in a different way. The paradox is that once we become more self-aware, strong in our knowledge of self, we can minimize our desire to personalize and make everything about self. Only then can we find our way back to the Garden of Eden, connected to everything around us.

It's Within You

Chapter 1

BEGINNING WITHIN

WRITTEN BY RABBI ARYEH WEINSTEIN

I can't change the direction of the wind, but I can adjust my sails to always reach my destination.

– JIMMY DEAN

YOU SEE SOMEONE CRYING, tears streaming down their face. Let's say it's your spouse or child. You might first wonder, "Why are they crying? Is it because their eyes hurt, or are they in pain?" While it's possible that this person just finished cutting an onion, the more likely scenario is that someone has hurt them physically or emotionally. So why are they crying if their emotions, not their eyes, are hurt? As we know, crying is a symptom of some deeper concern. This is true in most areas of our lives. When a deeper pain exists, we're often unable to identify it. It shows up as symptoms, such as tears, while the real issue remains hidden beneath the surface. We can run around and treat all the symptoms—which is often what we do in therapy and through the use of prescription medications—and this is, to some extent, effective and necessary for some medical conditions. But there's another way, a better way in most situations. When we dive deeper and get to the core of our issues—the pain stemming from our fundamental needs—we can start addressing the one thing that impacts everything else.

1

Imagine that the manager of a warehouse receives a delivery of 30 boxes, each weighing 100 pounds. The boxes are piled high on a pallet which was left at the curb. The manager now has to bring all of these boxes into the warehouse. He can do this in one of two ways. He can either carry in one box at a time, or he can rent a forklift to pick up and move the entire pallet at once. Which would be the wiser option? Well, if he carries in the boxes himself, he can get it done right away; he doesn't need anything other than his two hands. But taking 30 trips to get the job done without a forklift raises the likelihood that a box will drop and get damaged. Carrying the boxes in by hand will leave him exhausted and very likely injured from overexertion. Using a forklift, on the other hand, will take some time and resourcefulness; he'll need to find a way to get it to the warehouse. However, this option will help him remain safe and require only one effort to get all the boxes into the warehouse, at a much lower risk.

In life, we all have the same choice as this warehouse manager. Our first option is to deal with every issue and drama that shows up in our lives, one at a time. This can give us immediate relief, but similar issues usually wind up reappearing down the road. This option is almost guaranteed to leave us exhausted, since it involves fixing every symptom that shows up, without ever getting to the true nature of the problem. Many people who take this route end up getting too worn out to continue fighting, and they don't really solve anything. The other option is to get to the root cause of all our issues. This option requires a greater investment of time and energy, but the results are far better. We take this route by addressing the one thing that changes everything else.

We all seek inner peace, happiness and stability; yet no matter how hard we look, we don't seem to find it. When we don't find what we're looking for, it's usually a clear indication that we're looking in the wrong place. Most people spend the vast majority of their time feeling that the only way things will change in their lives is if their circumstances and the people they interact with would be different. "If only he'd be more thoughtful," they think. "If only I had different parents." "If only I got that job." But the truth is, there's only one person we can change: ourselves.

The good news is that when we begin changing ourselves, everything changes around us. There's a story about a woman who noticed that her neighbor's clothing, which was hung out to dry every day, was always dirty. She pointed this out to her husband: "Our neighbor can definitely use a new washing machine. Her clothes are always dirty." Then one day, they hired a window washer to clean their windows and, to their surprise, noticed that their neighbor's clothing was suddenly quite clean. They came to realize, of course, that their neighbor's clothing was never dirty; it was their filthy window creating this illusion all along. This story is a reflection of life. We're quick to point fingers at things outside of us, when the most productive place to point our finger is at ourselves. When we start to live by *beginning within,* the world around us suddenly takes on a very different appearance.

If someone spilled a cup of milk on you at the breakfast table, how would you feel? Imagine you'd just gotten dressed for work and then suddenly had to change out of your milk-stained clothing at the last minute. What would your emotional reaction be? Now imagine that you calmly told the person who spilled the milk, "It's OK. I've had my fair share of spills in life. I'll simply clean it up." That's powerful. That's peaceful. It shows acceptance of the event. Yet such behavior is pretty uncommon. I'll never forget the day I was driving in bumper-to-bumper traffic and slammed into the car in front of me. I had my whole family—all nine of us, at the time—in the car. Thank G-d, everyone was OK—except for our minivan, which was hardly drivable. The very first words my wife said to me were, "It's fine." This comment meant the world to me.

Despite this inconvenient and nearly devastating event, my wife didn't throw any anger or judgment at me.

Imagine if a friend or spouse told you they didn't like your outfit and you replied by thanking them for letting you know, without feeling the slightest bit offended. How about if you found out you had a flat tire just before leaving for work and, instead of it becoming the classic drama, you simply notified your boss and called someone to fix the tire. To some of you it might seem almost fantastical, non-human even, to live this way. You might be screaming, "You need to have some emotion in life!" Well, I happen to agree. That's what this book is all about: developing ourselves so we can spend more time with *healthy* emotions in response to reality, rather than getting consumed by negative emotions rooted in skewed perceptions of reality.

The journey you'll take with this book is the journey I'm personally on as well. When I began to realize how much I was struggling to love the people in my life, I knew I had a big problem on my hands. I realized something had to change when I noticed how defensively I responded to most people, which rarely yielded productive results. Simple conversations with my wife would often turn very personal, often ending in big arguments. I can still remember the time a community member—someone notoriously quick to complain—approached me to raise an issue. My instinctive response was to become defensive. Instead of addressing the issue he raised, I addressed my frustration with him, which only resulted in another issue. Of course, this didn't lead to anything productive; on the contrary, it was completely counterproductive.

Over time, I came to realize that I was always the focus of everything in my life. I measured everything according to how it affected me, what it said about me, whether it would inconvenience me, or how much it would cost me. One time I completely lost my cool with one of my children, who was only trying to express a need. I couldn't hear my child, because my ears were blocked by my inner chitter-chatter about how his request would affect me. Once again, all of the emphasis was on *me*. My child felt unheard. I—who am supposed to be their secure lifeline and biggest support—wasn't there for him when he needed me. When I came into awareness of this, I knew I had two choices: continue justifying this behavior, or start getting out of my own way so I can be there for others.

There's one incident from the time before I committed to becoming more aware of myself that really stands out for me. My wife and I were chatting with friends, and she shared something with them that I immediately contradicted. This humiliated her and, as she shared with me later, made her feel like she didn't have a trustworthy life partner. When I realized how much I'd hurt her, I began to introspect. I realized I was more concerned with what our friends would think about us than I was with my wife's dignity. Who was I married to, my wife or our friends? This incident made me feel like I'd emotionally betrayed my wife; surely this is not the kind of husband I want to be. I knew then that I couldn't continue down the same path. When I began observing how much of my life was dictated by people and things outside of me instead of from within, I began experiencing an entirely different life.

I want to be clear that the change I'm describing is not about blaming ourselves at all. This would be destructive, counterproductive, and unfair to ourselves. The reason we operate in ways that can be unproductive is that it's the primary behavior we've seen modeled by those around us. We shouldn't blame them either, though, as this is what they've seen modeled around them. Often, we haven't been taught a better way to deal with life, so we continue behaving the only way we know how. This book was designed to show you a new way—one that will help you live a life that isn't constantly dictated by the people and circumstances around you. Instead of having everything around you determine your state of mind and emotions, you become the source of your own thoughts and emotions.

The first step in this shift is to practice living by *beginning within*. It's important to remember that this process happens on a continuum; the goal is to make gradual but constant movement in the direction of healthier living. This process never ends, and we never get it 100% right. We don't seek to reach a goal of perfection but rather to continuously improve the way we process our lives, trying to muddle through the confusion of it all.

Remember that changing within is not only better for you, but for your personal relationships as well. I once read a blog post that brought me to tears. It was titled *How I Saved My Marriage* by Richard Paul Evans. In his heartfelt post, Evans described his marriage as one in which his and his wife's personalities clashed increasingly over time. When he eventually became a successful author, his fame only served to worsen the state of his marriage. Things were so difficult that Evans found it a relief to go on tour. There seemed to be no hope for him and his wife to find their way back to the peaceful relationship they once had. As time passed, each of them became more defensive and put up more walls; they even discussed divorce on several occasions.

One night, while Evans was on tour, he and his wife had another fight over the phone, and she hung up on him. He felt frustrated and alone, like he'd reached his limit. He broke down while taking a shower, not understanding why two good people couldn't just get along. He asked himself, "Why did I marry someone so different from me? Why won't she change?" Then, from somewhere deep inside, a wise idea came to him: "You can't change her; you can only change yourself."

Returning home, Evans was met with an ice-cold wife. That night, while lying in bed, another inspirational idea came to him.

When he awoke in the morning, he turned to his wife and asked, "How can I make your day better?" "You can't," was her angry reply. "Why are you asking?" "Because I mean it," he said. "I just want to know what I can do to make your day better." She paused for a moment and then replied, "You want to do something? Go clean the kitchen." Immediately, he got up from bed and gave the kitchen a thorough cleaning. The next day, he asked her the same thing. "Clean the garage," was her reply. The truth is, Evans didn't really have the time to spend two hours cleaning the garage, but he did it anyway. On the third day, when he asked his wife what he could do to make her day better, she got flustered and shot back, "Nothing! You can't do anything! Please, stop asking me!" All he said was, "I'm sorry, but I can't." She then asked, "Why are you doing this?" to which he replied, "Because I care about you and our marriage."

Evans did this every day for two weeks. One day during the second week, after his usual question, his wife broke down crying. She said, "I should be asking you the same question." He responded, "You should. But not now. Right now, I need to be the one to change. You need to know how much you mean to me." Like the walls of Jericho, their walls came tumbling down. Suddenly, two good people who never thought they would have a peaceful relationship again were experiencing the true depth of what marriage is. Their relationship wasn't saved by outside help; it was saved by one person in the marriage coming to the simple but profound realization that it's pointless to insist that others change. It's much more powerful and effective to look within ourselves and ask what we can change. Yes, the other person should be asking the same question; but that's for them to come to understand and do.

The one thing we all need to do is change ourselves. It's interesting to note that when Evans changed, his wife eventually changed as well. That's because when we start changing within, we become a source of inspiration and change for the people around us. It serves us to stop spending our time trying to change the people, things, and circumstances around us and instead start with the only thing we can change: ourselves. When we change ourselves, we suddenly start noticing the changes we've always wanted to see in the people and circumstances around us. As it turns out, it doesn't always take two people to fix a relationship; it only takes one—the one who is mature and willing enough to begin taking full responsibility and stop insisting that the other change.

Changing Within Versus Changing Circumstances

There's always an option to change the things in your life, even though it might be very difficult to do so. If you hate your car, hair, job, or weight, you can do something about it. Most people, when they're dissatisfied with the world around them, don't think about seeing how they can change from within; instead, they automatically start trying to change everything around them. We tend to believe that until things around us are different, we can't be emotionally sound or feel good about our lives. However, in reality, that very notion is what prevents us from making the changes necessary for us to live happy and fulfilling lives. When we use all our effort to look outside ourselves, we miss an opportunity to see what's within us. As an alternative to blaming our world, we can start by looking inside ourselves and asking, "How am I contributing to creating the world around me? In what ways are my thoughts and actions self-defeating and perpetuating the life I'm living? How do I benefit from the life I'm living, and why do I do the same automatic behaviors over and over again, even if they don't make me happy?" We must also reach a point when we acknowledge that while we can change the things in our lives, our efforts to change the circumstances and people around us have been ineffective.

I've found that until you change from within, life will keep handing you similar circumstances. At some point, you come to realize that you have a choice: You can react to life the same way you always have, wishing that annoying, difficult, horrible situation didn't happen, or you can choose to respond differently. Instead of always trying to change your outside world and complaining about the unfairness of it all, why not take the time to work on evolving from within? Imagine how different the world would be if we all did this.

What I mean by making changes from within is gaining the ability to manage your life and your stress levels, even under difficult circumstances. This kind of independence is accomplished by building who you are from the inside out, not the outside in. This leads to a type of inner resilience that lets you know you can meet, solve, and be with any circumstance you face. It means knowing your *sense of worth* on your own, without depending on others to make you happy or tell you who you should be. Accepting ourselves and changing unhelpful perceptions and behaviors allows us to find the strength we need to create a personalized sense of inner calm. It empowers us to see ourselves as separate *and* connected to others, allowing us to declare independence from circumstances that might once have dictated our moods, behaviors, and ideas about ourselves.

I know, I know. This all sounds good on paper, but putting it into practice is something else altogether. The truth is, it's more comfortable to focus on changing external factors than it is to focus on how *we* can change. Sometimes it's hard to avoid basing our personal value and worth on our external circumstances. We've all fallen into the trap of thinking things like, "I'll feel important once I get that fully loaded Lexus," or "My life will start when I get that raise and buy my dream home," or "I'll be happy when I find someone to marry." We truly believe that once we reach a particular external goal, then we'll be happy, once and for all. But as we've all found, once we finally reach the goal, that eternal happiness we so desired never appears. When this happens, most of us tend to move onto the next project or goal to prove to ourselves and others that we're worth something. But what we fail to see is that we were worthy all along.

A Nugget of Wisdom

The Hebrew word for face is *panim*. Like most Hebrew words, it is a multifaceted word that also means *within, pnimi*. This is because the one part of the body that most naturally reflects what is going on *within* a person is their face. As the saying goes, "It's written all over your face." Authenticity is expressed when our outside, our face, is consistent with our inside. An authentic life is lived when our external self is an expression of our internal self. When we live the reverse, bending our inner values to align with our outer image, we are introducing dishonesty. The spiritual and psychological school of thought that has influenced me most is Chabad Chassidic Philosophy. This philosophy has a yiddish adage for its adherents: "*Chabad munt pnimiyus*," Chabad demands living from within.

Summary

All of us can benefit from doing the work to change ourselves, instead of wasting our energy trying to change the people, things, and circumstances around us. When we put all our effort into looking outside, we're blocked from seeing what's within.

Activity

In this activity, you'll practice being an observer of your own life. When opportunities or situations arise, simply observe them. This will allow you to look at the situation from a more objective standpoint, instead of an emotional one, which will allow you to make better decisions. When observing a situation, seeing it for what it is, ask yourself: "What would I like to do in response?"

Take obstacles, situations, and interactions with people as an opportunity to check in and ask yourself who you are, who you want to become, and how you want to express *yourself.* Over time, you may notice that looking within and acting accordingly simply feels better than living from without.

Chapter 2

OUR FUNDAMENTAL NEED

WRITTEN BY RABBI ARYEH WEINSTEIN

Any love that is dependent on something—when the thing ceases, the love also ceases. But a love that is not dependent on anything never ceases.

– ETHICS OF OUR FATHERS, 5:16

THERE'S ONE FUNDAMENTAL NEED that, when we meet it, serves us well. It's so fundamental that, without necessarily realizing it, we're all desperately working to fulfill it. This fundamental need is our sense of worthiness—the knowledge that we are deserving, lovable, and indispensable. It's the need to know that who we are is different from what we do, and that our inherent self-worth is unchangeable. This need can only be met in one of two ways:

WITHOUT—Confirming our worthiness from outside sources, like people, things, and circumstances

WITHIN—Confirming our worthiness by knowing that we were intentionally put here by G-d for a unique purpose. It's the knowledge that says, "I am indispensable and worthy; otherwise I wouldn't be here."

Depending on external sources to confirm our self-worth sets us up for a lifetime of insecurity. On the other hand, when we recognize our intrinsic worthiness, our sense of security is solid and unwavering. Where we get our sense of self-worth affects practically all aspects of our lives.

Have you ever been a nervous wreck before going on a date, feeling unsure about whether the person will like you? Has your significant other ever said something that caused you to erupt emotionally and ruined the next 24 hours? Has anyone ever pointed out a stain on your clothing at the end of a long evening, leaving you humiliated about having walked around that way all night? Do you get frustrated when a friend or spouse loses their keys for the umpteenth time? Do you have a particular pleasure you indulge in when you get frustrated? Have you ever noticed yourself exaggerating or embellishing something to make yourself look just a little bit better? Have you lied about something to prevent an unnecessary confrontation?

I'm confident that practically everyone can relate to those situations in one way or another. Why is it that we get frustrated so easily? Why do we respond with anger? Why do we compliment people when we don't really mean it? Why do we minimize our failures and exaggerate our successes? Why do we get so defensive?

We can analyze each scenario and come up with hundreds of justifications for our actions under the circumstances; we're all good at excusing ourselves in this way. But what we don't tend to do is search for the reason behind those excuses. The truth is, there's one single reason that drives our responses in all of those situations: It's the desire to satisfy our inherent, foundational need to know that we are acceptable, worthy, and valuable. Some people call this self-esteem. It's getting through the day knowing that we're good enough, even if we don't totally feel like it. It's knowing we're still worthy even when we've made a mistake. It's recognizing that even though we have faults, weaknesses, and failures, we matter. We have inherent value simply because G-d created us. The more we implement this awareness into our psyche, the less affected we'll be by the people and circumstances around us.

Greg Baer, author of *Real Love*, shares two examples that clarify how our worthiness—or lack thereof—influences the way we respond to the events and people around us. Imagine that you only have two dollars left to your name. That's it. Then someone comes and steals those last two dollars from you. Naturally, you might feel furious. I mean, for heaven's sake, it's the only money you've got! Now imagine you have twenty million dollars and someone steals two dollars from you. Are you furious? Probably not. What's two dollars when you have twenty million? Nothing.

This example shows that it isn't the stealing of two dollars that makes us angry. If that were the case, we'd be just as angry in the millionaire scenario. The source of the anger is the lack of money; the initial scarcity before the petty theft is the true cause of pain. Similarly, when we barely have a sense of worthiness, an insult serves to take away the little bit we might have. Then, fear comes into play and we become overwhelmed by emotion—not because of the words that were said to us, but because of what we're already experiencing internally. When we're full of worthiness, other people's comments don't hurt us.

Imagine that you're sitting next to your future spouse and put your arm around their shoulder. How might they feel about such an embrace? They're likely to feel wonderful, of course. There's nothing like loving contact with someone you love. Now, imagine they just returned from the beach with a bad sunburn and, without knowing, you give them the same embrace. They're probably bound to jump back and scream. But why are they reacting that way? Not because your embrace hurts, but because they're *already in pain.* When someone is in pain, the smallest things can set them off.

The future spouse in that scenario screamed because of their own sunburn, their own issue. Likewise, if I lack a sense of worthiness and someone throws an insult at me, I'm going to feel hurt. But the source of the pain is not the insult; it's the existing wound that the insult provokes. If I have a strong sense of worthiness, I'm less sensitive to others' comments. I'm likely to hear the insult without being hurt by it.

A Jewish American serviceman who participated in the liberation of one of the concentration camps during the last days of World War II recounted his experience. He explained that before his platoon entered the camp, they were briefed by their commanding officer, who said, "What you're about to see is like nothing you've ever seen before." Referring to the food supplies the soldiers were planning to distribute to the hungry inhabitants of the cities they'd captured—which included Hershey's chocolate bars for the children—the officer issued a stern warning: "You must know, these people haven't eaten anything but scraps and morsels for years. As much as you may want to load them up with food, as much as you may wish to give the chocolate bars to the children here, you must not. Their systems would not be able to stand it. They could actually painfully die as a result. Our cooks and food experts know what to give them and how to ensure that they're slowly nourished back to health. Leave it to them."

As the soldiers entered the camp, the prisoners looked upon them as if they'd been sent from heaven. Then a child of skin and bones, barely alive, came up to this one particular soldier and begged him for food. The man's heart began to break. A starving, dying Jewish child was in desperate need right in front of him, and he couldn't pull out the food that was in his pack. He turned to the child, and in his broken American Yiddish, told him, "I don't have any food I can give you. But I know what I can give you. I can give you a hug."

In describing what happened next, the man writes, "I lifted this emaciated child and put my arms around him, and he put his thin bony arms around me. Tears began flowing down my cheeks. And then an incredible thing happened. Dozens of these children, barely alive, began flocking towards me, asking if they too could have a hug from this strong and proud Jewish liberator. Before long, there was a long line in front of me. They were standing there; not for a chocolate bar, not for a piece of bread, but just for a hug. After all the hatred and cruelty they'd encountered, just a little love and tenderness from a feeling and caring human being is all they wanted. And then even adults came over. They wanted a hug and support from someone who could show them some humanity. We silently hugged and cried together."

This touching story demonstrates the fundamental need of every human being. The extent to which this need is fulfilled has an enormous impact on the way we live our lives. We all need to know that we're worthy, that we have value, and that we're lovable and acceptable exactly as we are. Every human being needs to know that they have an indispensable purpose in this world.

Before moving to the Bucks County Pennsylvania community in 1999 to serve as a Rabbi, I received unsolicited advice from many people. I can only remember one piece of advice that was said to me, which I'll never forget. It was from Dr. Richard Sugarman, a Philosophy Professor at the University of Vermont. He said, "Make sure people know that they matter." At the time, I didn't realize the significance of his advice. However, I've come to realize since then that this is the core of any healthy, fully functioning human being.

A Choice Between Two Paths

There are two paths we can take toward feeling that we truly matter. The most common one, taken by the large majority of society, is the one that involves seeking applause and approval from others. The idea behind this one is that if other people embrace us, like us, and praise us, we get a sense of worth. It's proof that we matter. This is what I call *beginning without;* when we walk this path, we affirm our value based on people and things outside of us. The second path toward coming to know that we truly matter is the one that involves developing a deep understanding and belief that within us lies a unique purpose that we were put on this earth for, and that with every breath we take, G-d is reminding us of this purpose and assuring us that we matter. Whether we get applauded or not, and whether we've even begun fulfilling our purpose, our inherent value remains the same. This is what I call *beginning within.*

It is of the utmost importance for every single one of us to fully understand the difference between these two paths toward accepting ourselves, knowing that we matter, and recognizing that our existence is indispensable. The path we choose defines the way we approach almost everything in life, ultimately determining our quality of life. As we understand the paths more deeply, we can start to see how they define what we think, what we say, and how we behave.

Insecurity and Security

One fundamental difference between getting our self-worth from without versus within is the level of our confidence and security. When we choose the path of beginning without, we constantly seek acceptance and self-worth from others, ensuring that we remain insecure and self-conscious. Since we depend on others who are out of our control, we have no way of securing our self-worth and thus feel insecure all the time. We also become very self-conscious, as we measure everything people say and do according to whether it fulfills or denies our inherent need for self-worth. This leads us to constantly need other people to give us attention, affirm our importance, and tell us how good we are. The moment we stop hearing this from the world around us, we become desperate; once again, we have to scramble to find someone or something to give us the attention and approval we need. Our constant reliance on others for security reveals how dependent we are on external circumstances. Seeking our self-worth from others actually makes us feel more emotional and weak. When we live this way, we don't hold the reins of our own lives—others do.

People who choose the second path, that of beginning within, live with a foundation of security. They aren't self-conscious, because they don't depend on what others think to give them a sense of their worthiness. They don't need others to tell them how good they are. They don't need others to applaud them, nor do they rely on compliments or praise to let them know their inherent value. Their self-worth and acceptance come from the implicit knowledge that G-d created all of us for a purpose. Whether someone compliments or insults them, their emotional state isn't significantly impacted, because their inherent need to know they are acceptable and worthy doesn't come from others. While they pay attention to compliments and criticism to see what they can learn about themselves for the future, they don't take them personally. This is the most powerful way to live because it doesn't depend on people and situations out of our control. When we live this way, we only depend on the one thing which is very much within our control, and that's ourselves. Living on this path makes us strong, powerful, and independent people who hold the reins of our own lives.

The difference between the secure and insecure person tends to be most visible in situations where someone has to take responsibility. Under those circumstances, the secure person often rises like a lion to fulfill their purpose. The insecure person, on the other hand, won't always rise up. Their decision will depend on whether it will add or take away from the approval of the people around them. A secure person responds to the objective reality of the situation and makes decisions based only on what they believe to be the correct course of action. The insecure person, on the other hand, responds to their subjective reality of how people will perceive them.

If you've ever been disappointed by a leader or politician who hasn't risen to the occasion, you might now have some insight about why they didn't. They're likely insecure and averse to taking a position that isn't popular. That's why one important attribute of a real leader is the ability to step into responsibilities because it's the right thing to do, whether or not it's a popular move. There's a reason we get inspired by secure leaders; we see in them what we yearn to have within ourselves: independence, self-acceptance, and self-worth. The truth is, we're all leaders in our lives, our families, and our friendships. The more secure we make ourselves, the stronger our relationships can become and the better examples we can become for our children.

Arrogance and Humility

Beginning within is the vital first step toward becoming a secure person. And any conversation about security requires a clarification of the difference between *arrogance* and *humility*. Though most of us know arrogance when we see it, we often struggle to define exactly what it is. But all we need to do to is replace the word *insecurity* with *arrogance*. You see, arrogance is an attitude that masks tremendous insecurities hidden beneath the surface. It's an effort made by people who feel a driving need to prove to themselves and others that they're valuable and worthy.

Imagine that a high powered-attorney—a senior partner in his law firm—is sitting at his desk in the prized corner office. A woman who needs to speak to him about a legal issue she's dealing with arrives at the firm for a 9:00 am appointment with him. She shows up to his office, and the secretary says he's been waiting for her. She instructs the woman to go right inside. When the woman steps into his office, she finds him sitting with his feet up on the desk, reading a newspaper. Though it's clear he knows she's there, he doesn't look up at her and continues to read. After a couple of minutes pass, he puts down the newspaper, looks at her, and says, "How can I help you?"

Subtle occurrences like the one in this scenario happen in a multitude of ways, thousands of times a day. This attorney is a person who's worked all his life to demonstrate his worthiness and value to the world. He's sitting in an office that reflects his success and power. A simple, unassuming person walks into his office, and he *still* feels the need to assert his superiority. The new client isn't contesting his worthiness; in fact, by reaching out to him for help, she's demonstrating how much she values him. Yet, the lawyer still feels the need to emphasize his importance. Where does this come from? The answer is insecurity. And it's this very insecurity that presents itself as arrogance.

Once we're aware of the relationship between arrogance and insecurity, we can see the connection clearly. The moment we see someone acting arrogantly, we can be sure it's coming from insecurity. It's the reason they feel the need to assert their value to everyone. In an interesting way that many people might fail to see, the lawyer is demonstrating a need for his new client to approve of him so that he can feel worthy. That's the subtle, unspoken story of what's going on in this scenario. Imagine, after all his years in law school and all the years he's spent practicing law, he's still the same insecure person. This is truly a human tragedy. One thing this lawyer hasn't learned is that if he wants to feel his worthiness, he has to stop getting it from external sources, like the office he has or the car he drives. Once he learns to acknowledge his inherent worthiness from *within,* his insecurity and arrogance can transform.

Humility is a commonly misunderstood word. Most people associate it with weakness, but here's the surprising truth: humility breeds unbelievable strength. You see, humility is the behavior of a secure person. It's the lawyer who's welcoming, down to earth, and feels no need to assert himself because his self-worth comes from *within.* To access the strength that comes from beginning within, it's important to be clear about the distinctions between security and insecurity, arrogance, and humility.

Now, there's a form of humility I'm going to refer to as *false humility.* This appears when someone acts humble but doesn't think or feel this way. False humility is the person who receives a compliment and waves it off, saying, "I'm not that good," while internally riding a high and thinking to himself, "Yeah, I really am good." This act of humility is just that: an act.

At this point, you might be wondering how to tell whether someone's humility is genuine or false. The truth is, you may not always be able to spot the difference; doing so depends on your ability to read other people. When it comes to your own relationship with humility, what's most important is whether you're truly humble or putting on an act of false humility while actually feeling arrogantly self-assured. Being aware of this is really important because it serves as an indicator of whether you're living from without or from within.

Understanding Internal Worthiness

When attempting to understand our internal worthiness, it's vital to remember that we don't need to find value; we were given value when we were given life. It's not about getting what we want out of life, it's about recognizing our purpose and being true to who we were created to be. Once we understand this clearly, we're on our way to finding *peace* and *happiness*. And who doesn't want peace and happiness? Not only do we deserve to feel these things and know our worthiness without question, we have an *obligation* to; it's our primary purpose to gain an understanding of what we already possess. It's easy, sometimes, to forget our worthiness when we experience the misfortunes of life, or when others try to convince us through their words or actions that we aren't worth much. Knowing our intrinsic value is an indispensable aspect of actualizing the potential within all of us.

The concepts in this chapter are often forgotten, or never even realized to begin with. One reason is that the world can sometimes seem like a cruel place. Loved ones can be taken from us without warning; accidents can change our lives forever; a relationship that was once deeply comforting can turn into a major stressor. We go through heartache, pain, disaster. Seemingly cruel people crush our spirits or challenge the way we see ourselves. Ever changing circumstances, which start shaping us at an early age, alter the way we see the world—a world that can sometimes seem safe, but more often feels uncertain. The gift of life might not feel like such a gift at all when we encounter the difficulties it brings.

No matter how much your circumstances change, if you understand your value and have a core sense of self, the knowledge of your worthiness will serve as an anchor in even the most horrible of circumstances. It can be your shelter in the worst of storms. In an unpredictable world you'll know that no matter what, the emotions will pass, and you'll find yourself once again.

Your core self—which is separate from all external influences—won't rise and fall like stock market prices; instead, it will remain unshaken and forever whole. This is what it's like to live with the basic knowledge of your human worth.

You might be wondering, "What does it mean to have an internal sense of worthiness?" Simply put, it means that you understand your unconditional human worth. You know your value and significance, and you recognize that your inner self is priceless and irreplaceable. You know, to your core, that you're just as important as anyone else. I know that sounds a bit like motivational talk and positive affirmation without any evidence. You might be thinking, "You don't even know me. How can you say that?" The thing is, I'm not saying this to compliment you or make you feel better about yourself. I'm saying it because I believe all humans are infinite, eternal, and unwaveringly valuable. While some have more fame, money, or athletic ability, others are better at social skills and connecting with others. In spite of our many different strengths and capabilities, we're all equally worthy as human beings.

Throughout this book, we'll be using terms like *inner self, core self, true self, and spiritual self*—all different words to express the same idea. Like a newborn baby, the *self* is essentially perfect and whole; it's complete as is, but not yet totally developed. When a baby is born, we know its value and are easily able to love it, regardless of whether it's rich, famous, or bound to be an athletic all-star. That baby is lovable, beautiful, and full of potential. And so are we.

Over time, the baby that was born perfect, whole, and complete—possessing the same core self it was born with—may become overwhelmed by external circumstances. Over time, this human may begin to confuse their worth with their accomplishments. Like dust covering a window that looks out on a scenic landscape, some external factors can bury the beautiful view of what's beyond the surface. Children who grow up in a harsh and critical environment may conceal their core self, making it difficult for them to understand and see their value. But the reverse is also true. When we receive love from others, it's easier for us to see our value, too. We often do this by showing off a special skill we've developed as a way to prove our worthiness to others. However, it's essential for us to remember that this is a way of changing the way we *experience* our inherent self-worth and not a means of generating that self-worth.

In my work, I've met with many successful people who admit that they still aren't happy. What I say in response is what I've been saying in this chapter: It isn't possible to gain internal self-worth through personal achievements or other external rewards—because it already exists! Instead of having all our worth rely on external rewards, we must separate our core self from external factors and start living lives that begin within.

A Nugget of Wisdom

There is nothing in this world that is absolute and constant. Have you ever wondered why? It's because anything that is *dependent* cannot be entirely reliable. Since everything was created, it's all inherently dependent on its creator. Therefore, when we base our value on worldly accomplishments or other people, our value cannot be absolute and constant. The only entity that is independent, upon which all else relies, is Almighty G-d. When we acknowledge that our life is from G-d, we know that in every breathing moment, G-d is reminding us that we matter. This value is absolute and constant.

Summary

Your worth is already established. It's there whether you're relaxing or working, whether you're on your best behavior or your worst. Your core self is more than your achievements. It's more than your titles, awards, or anything else you get from the outside world. Your main challenge is to understand this and experience the joy that comes with recognizing our implicit worthiness.

The most common reason we tend to turn to other people and things to gain a sense of worthiness is that we're self-conscious and insecure. This leads to arrogance and dependence on others for our most fundamental need. It's what creates failed leaders who are unable to act when they should, for fear that they'll fall out of favor. Hopefully, you've begun to notice how much your emotional state is affected by the people, things, and circumstances around you. To recap some main points:

1. We all have an inherent human need to know we're worthy.
2. There are only two ways for us to find worthiness: from without or from within.
3. Finding worthiness from without leads to insecurity and arrogance.
4. Finding worthiness from within creates a choice of being secure and humble.
5. Attempting to get worthiness from without creates dependence.
6. Attempting to get worthiness from within makes us free and independent.

Activity

Question 1: From 1-10—with 1 being the lowest and 10 being the highest—which number would reflect how much of your life is lived from within? Simply choose a number.

1	2	3	4	5	6	7	8	9	10

Question 2: Write down one way your life would be different if you lived more from within.

_____

_____

The objective of this activity is to make us more aware of how people and circumstances affect us. We're not trying to fix anything; we only want to become aware of what's happening.

Reflect on your day, and identify one event or interaction with another person, in which something they said or did triggered a negative emotion or response from you. Write down the event or interaction that triggered your negative emotion or response, then answer these questions on the back of this page:

- What was the feeling or response triggered within you?
- Did you consciously decide to have this feeling, or was it an immediate reaction to the event?
- Was your feeling triggered from within or from your thoughts about how others would react?

Here are Some Examples:

Example 1:
- My boss told me he didn't like the way I prepared the report.
- I felt hurt.
- I immediately felt this emotion when he said he didn't like the report.
- My feeling was triggered from others, by his comment

Example 2:
- My child hit me.
- I got angry.
- The moment after he hit me I felt the emotion immediately.

- My feeling was triggered from without; it was triggered by his hitting me.

Example 3:

- My husband told me my dress was too casual for the event
- I got angry.
- I felt this the moment after he told me.
- My feeling was triggered from others, by his comments.

Write down the event or interaction that triggered your negative emotion or response.

_____

_____

_____

What emotion or response was triggered in you?

_____

_____

Did you consciously decide to have this feeling, or was it an immediate reaction to the event?

_____

_____

Was your feeling triggered from within or from without?

_____

_____

_____

_____

Chapter 3

THE TRUE YOU

WRITTEN BY RABBI ARYEH WEINSTEIN

*Patterning your life around other's opinions
is nothing more than slavery.*

— LAWANA BLACKWELL

MAGINE SOMEONE'S DROWNING in the middle of the ocean. They so desperately need oxygen that they'll literally do anything to breathe. They can't think about or focus on anything else. This person's life is on the line, and they'll do anything to save it. This desperation makes drowning victims a threat to anyone trying to rescue them. They're likely to instinctively grab at anything to help stabilize themselves so they can breathe. They might even push their rescuer down to get themselves up. Not because they want to harm the person saving them, of course, but because their efforts to stay alive make them oblivious to everyone else—even those who are key to their survival.

Something exactly like this happens within all of us. We drown when we don't have the emotional oxygen we need to function as vibrant, healthy individuals. This oxygen is the knowledge and awareness that we're acceptable and worthy. When we don't inherently know this, we get desperate. Just like a drowning person, we'll do almost anything, even to those we love, in order to confirm our worthiness. This becomes the driving force behind a life spent in constant search of acceptance from the world outside. Can you imagine the tragedy of someone spending 80 years drowning? That's a long time to experience fright, desperation, and pain. But that's precisely what it's like to live dependent on external sources of validation.

In our current, self-help-obsessed world, we're surrounded by many gurus teaching us how to create the impression that we're strong, confident, independent, and self-made. I'm skeptical of this particular message, and I hope you will be too because putting on an act doesn't allow us to address our deeper challenges. Learning to give a firm handshake and look someone in the eyes doesn't give us true confidence. Though they're useful techniques, they only provide a temporary fix or address a specific interaction. The real solution lies at the core of what we're lacking and what we need: *knowing our inherent self-worth.* As long as we try to gain approval from the world, we won't resolve our fundamental core issue.

When we don't know that we're worthy and acceptable on our own, we live like we're drowning all the time. We'll do anything to feel worthy, even if it hurts the people around us, whom we otherwise love. We'll say and do hurtful things, acting in unhealthy ways to find a sense of worthiness.

Hiding

The first way to begin getting our worthiness from within and not without is by learning to adopt behaviors that well-functioning people use. It is also by identifying our unhealthy behaviors that we need to eliminate. There's one classic tactic we subconsciously use to gain a sense of worthiness from others: hiding. Many of us subconsciously believe that if we hide a part of ourselves from others, they'll accept us and deem us worthy.

Here are a few common scenarios. As you read them, see if you can spot the common intention being expressed in all of them:

1. I call my spouse to say I'll be home in 15 minutes when I know I won't get there for at least half an hour.

2. I tell my friend that what they did is fine when I'm really not okay with it at all.

3. Someone tells me they got offended by something I said. I respond with, "I can never say the right thing to you."

4. I laugh at a supervisor's joke, even though I found it offensive.

5. When someone asks me how much my shoes cost I make them sound more expensive than they are.

6. I tell a colleague how much I loved their presentation, even though it bored me to death.

7. I get angry and yell at my spouse or friend, who suggested that how I handled something wasn't proper.

We often rationalize common scenarios like these as ways of defusing situations or preventing small issues from becoming bigger. Yet, when we look a little closer, we can see a common theme. The behaviors reflected in these examples can, over time, become a way of life. Without realizing it, they make it more and more difficult to be in close and intimate relationships. When we behave this way, we not only lose touch with others but with ourselves as well. We hide, intentionally concealing our true selves while mistakenly believing it's benefiting everyone involved.

Let's revisit each scenario with a brief explanation:

1. I call my spouse and say I'll be home in 15 minutes when I know I won't get there for at least half an hour. *By not*

speaking the truth as I know it, I'm clearly trying to hide from my spouse. My hope is that they won't be upset with me—or, in other words, that I won't fall out of favor with them.

2. I tell my friend what they did is fine when I'm really not okay with it at all. *I'm hiding my true feelings so my friend will accept me and I don't have to risk them being upset with me.*

3. Someone tells me they were offended by something I said. I respond with, "I can never say the right thing to you." *I'm making myself a victim and hiding from taking responsibility for hurtful words I said.*

4. I laugh at a supervisor's joke, even though I found it offensive. *I'm hiding my true feelings to appear easygoing and avoid rejection.*

5. When someone asks me how much my shoes cost I make them sound more expensive than they are. *I deliberately hide the truth to make myself look better and gain approval.*

6. I tell a colleague how much I loved their presentation, even though it bored me to death. *Again, I deliberately hide my true feelings and flatter someone to gain approval.*

7. I get angry and yell at my spouse or friend, who suggested that how I handled something wasn't proper. *I'm hiding behind my anger and intimidation so I won't have to deal with the real issue.*

We pay an enormous price when we hide. If we want to have genuine, intimate relationships, we have to show up. The more we show of ourselves, the more available we are to others; the more we hide, the less present we are to our relationships. No matter how hard others might try, they can't get close to us if we're too busy hiding.

Many of us think that by hiding, we'll get others to like us more, which will sustain or even strengthen our relationships with them. But the truth is, hiding makes it impossible for us to get close. By being ourselves, even when that doesn't look so good, we make it possible for true connection to happen.

When I tell you that I won't be at the restaurant for another half hour, even though I know you won't be happy about it, I'm showing up for you. You know it's me you're dealing with, and not some phony facade. If we're having a conversation and I tell you that I have a different perspective instead of simply agreeing with you, you know that I'm really showing up in our relationship and not just trying to fit in. When I don't use anger to shut down a conversation about something upsetting I did, and instead listen to you voice your dissatisfaction, I'm showing that I'm present and available to you.

Here's a simple equation that can help you remember this concept:

HIDING = SEEKING

SHOWING UP = FINDING

If you continuously hide from the people around you, you'll continuously seek close relationships without finding them. You can't get close, after all, if you're always hiding. If, however, you continuously work on showing up in your relationships, you'll continuously find the close relationships you desire. Presence is far more powerful than charisma. Charismatic people can draw others to them, but unless they're truly showing up, their relationships will be shallow and short-lived.

When we hear public speakers share something vulnerable about themselves, we feel much more connected to them. Their willingness to show up compels us. Vulnerability is scary; we're terrified of what people will think if they see who we truly are. But the reality is, it's this very vulnerability that inspires and attracts others. When people show the courage to express their true selves, the connections they build are limitless. This book will teach you how to take slow steps to express your vulnerability and reap the enormous benefits that come with it.

Before you can maximize the power of vulnerability in your relationships, you must start by seeing the ways you're hiding. There are several classic behaviors we use to hide from others. Pay close attention, and see which ones you identify with most.

Lying. This is the one behavior that incorporates all other forms of hiding. We lie because we want to hide the truth behind a false reality and avoid consequences. I can still remember the day my mother came downstairs and saw the glass of a picture frame shattered. She demanded to know who did it. Though I was the one who broke it, I joined my siblings in denying it. Why did I lie? To stay in my mother's good graces, of course. I created a false reality to look good in front of her.

Exaggerating and Minimizing. Very often, we lie in much more subtle ways. One way we do this is by exaggerating or minimizing the truth. Have you ever found yourself embellishing an accomplishment or downplaying a failure? Most of us have. We do it simply to make ourselves look a little better, because we measure our value and self-worth by what we do, not who we are. We fear that others won't accept us or find us worthy, so we hide by presenting things differently than the way they are. Imagine if someone asked you how many people attended your workshop and you said 40 when it was really 30. Why did you need to add an additional 10 people? You might report that you made $5,000 from a business deal when you only made $4,000. Why add that $1,000? We often dismiss these subtleties as insignificant, but they're motivated by a very clear intention: to make ourselves look better to others.

Flattering. Flattery—excessive and insincere praise used to further one's own interests—is another form of hiding. We do this in an effort to stay in people's good graces and have them approve of us. Some people lead with flattery in their efforts to secure relationships, heaping on the compliments so they don't have to deal with reality.

Seeking Praise. It feels wonderful to earn someone's praise. And many of us were raised to go through life seeking it through our actions and accomplishments. Our decisions are dictated by what others want us to do, not by what we believe we should do. Seeking praise can actually turn into an addiction if it replaces exploration of our own needs and aspirations.

Gratitude and thanks are two other forms of praise. Have you ever given someone a beautiful gift, then resented them for not thanking you appropriately? Why did you give the gift? Was it for them, or was it for you to hear how much they appreciate you? Ideally, a gift is given for the benefit of the other person. But when we have the expectation of receiving thanks, we give the gift to meet our own need for appreciation. The focus is primarily on ourselves. When we live our lives *beginning without,* this is the primary motivation behind our gift-giving. I know some of you might be thinking, "Look, when someone does something that's clearly wrong, like not saying thank you when I give them a gift, my conscience gets me upset. This is how any decent person would feel." But let me ask you this: When I give someone a gift and they don't thank me, why don't you get upset about it? Why do you only get upset when it happens to you? Catch my drift? This goes a lot deeper than a conscience. It's about our desire to know that we're worthy and valuable.

Respect. Some people live their lives demanding respect. When they don't feel respected, they're immediately reminded that they feel unworthy. Of course, there are times when respect is due, but people aren't obligated to give it to us. When I get angry about feeling disrespected, I make it clear that I'm dependent on respect from others. Now you might say, "No, my sense of justice tells me to be upset when people don't act properly." I hear you, and I've felt the same way in many situations. However, I want you to know that our anger isn't coming from our sense of justice. We know this from the fact that when others are disrespected, we won't get nearly as upset as we do when the disrespect is directed toward us. We only get upset when *we* feel disrespected. That's because we're desperately relying on others for our sense of worthiness; when someone doesn't treat us with respect, we feel like we don't matter.

Power. Some people aren't too gentle; they use power to force others to recognize and affirm them. Instead of learning to access their worthiness from within, they use power to seek it from without. They deflect from focusing on their own issues by imposing them onto others. This is a form of control. Of course, it's quite ridiculous for us to force others to tell us we're worthy, but in our desperation, that's exactly what we do. If they aren't careful, teachers and parents can easily do this with children. Unhealthy and extreme dynamics of power and control in relationships can lead one partner to use anger as a way to intimidate their spouse to serve them and make them feel worthy.

Apologizing. Often, all we want is to minimize criticism and maximize acceptance from the people in our lives. One way we do this is by pacifying them, agreeing with them all the time, and apologizing for things that aren't our fault—all to remain in their good graces and feel loved, accepted, and worthy.

Victimhood. Another classic way of acquiring a sense of acceptance is by treating ourselves like victims. We blame those around us for our plight, in hopes that they'll feel bad for us and accept us. Or, if we're lucky, others will shower us with love to make us feel better. Again, we're doing everything possible in a desperate attempt to get someone to tell us we're acceptable, all the while knowing—subconsciously, at least—that if we have to victimize ourselves to gain it, their acceptance isn't that genuine.

All of these forms of hiding exist within the context of our relationships. And there are tons of other ways we operate in relationships in order to get a sense of worthiness. We pursue money with the belief that once we have a certain amount, people will respect us. We dress a certain way so that we might be told how beautiful we are. We score well on tests, win competitions, buy expensive cars, and earn fancy degrees in the hope of gaining a sense of worthiness and acceptance from others.

Gaining Self-Awareness

So how do we stop hiding to feel worthy? As it goes with all forms of change, the first step is becoming aware. The previous chapter's activity was focused on creating awareness of what triggers our feelings. This chapter's activity will focus on becoming aware of things we say and do to gain acceptance from others. We must first become aware of our behaviors and the motivation behind them. A good place to start is by taking a moment at the end of each day to reflect on one thing you said or did based on a need to feel worthy. This powerful and courageous first step will help you begin to develop greater awareness. Later in the book, you'll learn new behaviors that will anchor you to the source of worthiness that exists within you.

When we think about living from without as a form of drowning all the time, we can understand why we tell white lies, exaggerate and minimize, patronize, hide behind anger, assert our power, and act like victims. We believe that these tactics will give us the oxygen we need to breathe.

You might be thinking, "So what? If this is how I get my worthiness, and it works, let it be." But here's what we must realize. Not only does it not work, it *can't* work; and worse, it becomes the root of all of the negative experiences in our relationships. We treat those relationships as transactional, and our worthiness and acceptance only last as long as we keep making payments.

There are two primary characteristics of seeking worthiness from without:

1. It's never-ending, turning us into perpetual seekers.

2. It's like taking illegal drugs, binging on food, or drinking alcohol. It's a quick fix that provides us immediate but short-lived relief that only leads to greater pain later.

In life, it's best to always take the longer-shorter way—the one that's more work up front but makes life much easier down the road. The shorter-longer way might be easier and more fun at first, but we pay a big price for it later on. Shortcuts always catch up to us.

This can be true in our most important relationships. Let's use dating as an example. If two people, after dating for a while, only share ideas and opinions they know they'll agree about, they aren't truly showing up for the encounter. They aren't bringing their full selves to the dates. Why are they doing this? Well, by now you know it's because they want to be accepted. Imagine that these two people go on to get married, only to discover years later that they don't really know each other. How did this happen? Because they spent the dating process hiding. How did it serve their marriage for them to avoid showing up? Disastrously! The only way to spare it, at that point, is to keep hiding to keep things smooth and easy.

Hiding is a heavy burden for us to carry. In fact, most people who go down the road of seeking worthiness from without become completely exhausted by the constant need to feed their unquenchable desire for worthiness. When they get burnt out by it, different areas of their lives begin to fall apart. By reading this book and applying what you're learning, you'll be doing some hard work up front, but dodging disastrous results later on.

Let's review what we've learned so far:

Living from Without	Living from Within
Immediate results that quickly diminish	Slow, lasting results
Transactional	Transformational
Perpetual seeking	Unshakable acceptance
Living to gain acceptance	Living to fulfill purpose
Constant reminder of lack of self-worth	Constant self-assurance
Victimhood	Freedom
Shame	Vulnerability
Creating distance	Creating connection
Body	Soul

A Nugget of Wisdom

The Hebrew word for world is *olam,* a derivative of the word *he'elam,* which means hidden. This is because the very nature of the world is its hiding of a deeper reality, its Creator. This is, in fact, the entire purpose of the universe. A realm that does not naturally recognize its source coming to this recognition on its own. This is because the deepest recognition one can have is when discovered by oneself, not the one imposed by another. This is just another example of the value of beginning *within.* When we use a battery powered device, we always remain aware of the device's dependence on the battery. While the world is equally dependent on its source for existence, it successfully hides its dependence. This is why we can feel immortal for so many years and why we comfortably put our trust in things that are so unreliable. Hiding is the inherent challenge of our world. When we pursue more truthfulness, not only do we drastically improve our personal lives, we actually repair the very fabric of the universe.

Summary

Living from without keeps us in an endless cycle of *buying* approval from others. We spend our time seeking acceptance and compromising who we are so we can be who others want us to be. We learn to hide and hold back to maintain relationships, but all it does is make it impossible for us to get closer to others. It keeps us from ever getting to show our true selves.

Activity

The objective of this exercise is to *make you more aware of the things that you think, say, or do to gain acceptance from others.*

The point isn't to fix anything, only to become more aware of what's happening. Reflect on your day and identify one event or interaction in which you thought, said, or did something to gain the acceptance of another, no matter how trivial it might seem. Write down what you said or did, then answer this question:

- What were you hoping to gain from this thought, statement, or action?

Here are Some Examples:

Example 1:

- When my spouse told me that she was upset that I made her late, I made myself the victim, thereby not taking responsibility and hiding.
- I said, *"Everything's always my fault,"* instead of acknowledging my actions and apologizing. I was hoping she would feel bad and stop being upset with me.

Example 2:

- When my spouse asked me who I was talking to, I lied.
- I said it was my boss instead of admitting that it was a friend he doesn't approve of. I was hoping to avoid a confrontation with him and maintain his acceptance.

Example 3:

- I angrily insisted that my employee do it my way and not their way.
- When my employee proposed a different way of doing something, I angrily said, *"This is my business, and things will get done my way."* I was hoping to use the intimidation of anger to force them to acknowledge my importance as the boss.

Write down what you said or did.

_____

_____

_____

_____

_____

_____

What were you hoping to gain from it?

_____

_____

_____

_____

_____

_____

_____

Chapter 4

YOUR POWER SPACE

WRITTEN BY RABBI ARYEH WEINSTEIN

Between stimulus and response, there is a space.
In that space is our power.

– VIKTOR FRANKL

HOPE THAT BY COMPLETING THE ACTIVITY at the end of the previous chapter, you've begun to see how hiding creates distance from others. It's been said that knowing the problem is half the solution; if this is true, we're already halfway there! In all of the unhelpful behaviors we've discussed, who is it that we're most concerned with in our interactions? If we're honest, the answer most of the time is *ourselves*. Like the drowning person who unintentionally pulls their rescuer underwater to save themselves, we can all get so singularly focused in our desperation that we harm others and ourselves in the process. To shift this pattern, we must stop making ourselves our main concern. By doing so, we initiate a useful self-perpetuating cycle: the less consumed we are with ourselves, the less desperate we feel; the less desperate we feel, the easier it is to respond to life and others in *effective* ways.

I want to clarify what I mean by all of this because it can easily be misconstrued as suggesting we must only think of others instead of ourselves. There's no doubt we must consider our needs and desires as well. Doing so makes it possible for us to take care of our bodies, maintain our emotional health, and make sure we aren't in danger. It's also necessary that we care for ourselves so we can care for others. The problem comes when we focus so much on ourselves that we lose perspective in our relationships, failing to see the bigger picture. We get defensive, consumed by concerns about how everything in the relationship affects and reflects upon us. This happens when the things we do for ourselves become about ourselves. When we learn to expand our focus, we can start to see other people's perspectives and context as well. We gain the ability to be *objective*, getting closer to reality instead of being boxed in by our subjective experience. This gives us the power to address others' fears and concerns as well as our own, which serves as a tremendous source of strength for our most important relationships. Imagine how powerful you'd be if someone hysterically accused you of something, and instead of getting *defensive*, you simply focused on becoming curious about their perspective.

What we usually discover when we listen to others' concerns and viewpoints is that doing so expands our perspective. I can't tell you how many times I've been sure that my wife is absolutely wrong about something, only to later discover by listening intently to her that her perspective makes sense. These repeated experiences with her and others have humbled me to always try and listen to the other person, no matter how convinced I am that I know better.

Let's do a fun and eye-opening activity. On the next page you'll see what's referred to as **Shepard's Rotated Tables**. Take a look at both of the tables, and make note of which one looks longer to you. Now take a tissue or piece of paper and place it over the table that appears longer. Draw an outline of the top of the table, so you end up with a rectangular shape on your tissue or paper. Next, take the outline, turn it ninety degrees, and place it over the other table.

I hope you're as amazed by the result as I was when I first did this. When I first considered which table looks longer, I suspected that they were the same size, but my eyes refused to see it that way. Then I drew the outline of the table that appeared longer and placed it over the other table. Seeing that they were, in fact, the same exact size was shocking. No matter how hard I try to see it another way, the table on the left always appears longer to me. Even though the truth has been revealed, my eyes still can't see it.

This exercise made me question how I determine what reality is. I now have conclusive evidence that what I see isn't necessarily the way things are. Just as our eyes are absolutely sure that the tables differ in size, so we are often convinced that our way of seeing things is the true and only way. When we understand that perception isn't reality, we develop a little bit of humility, knowing that we can't look at anything in a purely objective way. We're inherently biased by our beliefs, orientations, and past experiences. So, no matter how convinced we might be about something, we must always open our minds to the fact that things might not be what they seem (The exception to this would be divine knowledge). There might just be another perfectly reasonable perspective. The trick to being more objective is knowing that we're subjective beings who can never see things exactly as they are. In a wonderfully paradoxical way, acknowledging this actually brings us closer to the truth.

Perception Versus Reality

I've always been curious about the nature of personal bias. There's a story I'm particularly drawn to about a great Jewish mystic and spiritual master named Reb Zushe, whose disciples once found him alone and distraught, pacing around his home repeating, "Where is Zushe? Where is Zushe?" The disciples were concerned, believing their master had lost his mind. When he found an opportunity, one of the disciples asked him, "What did you mean by your question, 'Where is Zushe?' Why would a person ask himself, 'Where am I?'" The master responded, "One day I'm going to die. You will walk in and find my body here on the floor, and I will be exactly as I am right now—the same flesh, the same bones, the same countenance. Yet, you will be crying, 'Holy master, why did you leave us? Holy master, where did you go?' But I will not have gone anywhere. I will be right before you. However, you understand that I, Zushe, am not a body. My true self is my soul. It will be the true me that you will be crying for. After thinking about this, I considered that now must be the time for me to discover the real me, not when my soul has already left my body. This is why I asked, 'Where is Zushe?' I have begun looking for my soul, the real me."

Understanding this story can help us see that our fundamental issue with worthiness comes from the way we identify ourselves. It's rooted in the fact that we're all made up of matter and spirit, body and soul. The body is born, and the body dies. The soul, however, is eternal. Our temporary body is the part of us that constantly seeks affirmation to know that it's worthy. Why? Because it knows that it's only temporary—and how valuable can something temporary be? Our soul, being eternal, knows its inherent worth.

Our body is our external self, and our soul is our internal self. The body, in its desperation for worthiness, is biased in all situations to see only what will bring it worthiness. *This is what many people call selfishness.* Everything revolves around ourselves because we're so desperate to feel worthy. This is the reason we see, hear, and experience things differently from the way they are. Our body never seeks to know the truth; it only seeks to know how situations will affect *it*. This is the reason why the exact same thing can be said to two people, and both walk away having heard something completely different. We process what we hear through our individual filters, and what comes out the other side becomes a distorted version of reality. The soul has no agenda; it's inherently secure with its own worthiness and can, therefore, experience reality for exactly what it is, without putting any particular spin on it. The body never sees reality clearly, and the soul always maintains a clear vision. So how do we balance it all? How do we separate truth from subjective experience? How do we get closer to our soul's perceptions of reality?

Consider this story. A couple is cleaning up after dinner. The husband is washing the dishes, and the wife is drying them. After the husband washes a particular dish and hands it to his wife, she comments, "Honey, this dish is still dirty." The husband responds, "If you don't like the way I wash the dishes, you can wash them yourself!" Let's take a closer look at what happened here. The wife expressed a simple, objective observation: the dish is still dirty. Anyone who looks at this dish will see that it's dirty. In hearing his wife's observation, the husband could simply have said, "Oh, let me rewash the dish." He didn't respond that way, however, because he wasn't responding to the reality of the situation; he was responding to his *biased interpretation* of the meaning he attached to his wife's words. Most likely, he interpreted that his wife thinks he doesn't know how to wash dishes, which left him feeling devalued and unworthy. He then responded to that interpretation by defending himself. His wife, on the other hand, was completely unaware of his interpretation and, therefore, couldn't understand why he responded the way he did. The inherent bias of our bodies, which lead us to feel insecure about our worthiness, trickles down into the way we respond to simple, everyday occurrences like a dirty dish.

Checking Into Reality

Let's come back to an important question: How do we see reality for what it truly is, without shading it with our biased view? To answer this, I'll share with you a very basic process that I call the **checking into reality** exercise. You can use it in any situation you find yourself in, to avoid personalizing what's going on and begin seeing reality as objectively as possible. If we put most of our experiences in a slow-motion sequence, we can break them down into five steps:

Event – Judgment – Feeling – Space – Response

The quote I opened this chapter with, from Viktor Frankl's book *Man's Search for Meaning*, offers a powerful frame for the **checking into reality** exercise. He says, "Between stimulus and response, there is a space. In that space is our power to choose our response. In our response lies our growth and our freedom." When we learn to *slow down* and observe the five stages inherent in all our experiences, we can uncover the space between the event and our response to it.

1. **The Event.** This is what actually occurs, without any form of added interpretation. The event is the objective occurrence. In the example of the dishwashing couple, the husband handed his wife a dish that he'd just washed. She told him the dish was still dirty. That was the objective event.

2. **The Judgment.** This is how we interpret the event. Our interpretations are personal and typically driven by our biases and past experiences. The husband in our example judged that his wife said he doesn't know how to wash the dishes.

3. **The Feeling.** This is when our judgment of the event triggers our feelings about it. The husband's judgment of his wife's words—"I don't know how to wash dishes"—led to his feelings of unworthiness, which awakened his instinctive desperation for emotional oxygen.

4. **The Space.** A powerful space exists between our feelings and our response. In this moment, which only needs to last a few seconds or less, we have the opportunity to consider whether our judgment is absolute truth or a defensive, biased story. This space allows us to ask ourselves questions like, "Is my interpretation true? Even if my interpretation is true, why does it concern me so deeply? Does this event define my worthiness?"

5. **The Response.** This is the action we take. Our natural response will be based on how we feel. The husband reacted defensively, which is no surprise considering his judgment and feelings. He probably wasn't aware of the fact that his strong feelings came from his insecurities, and not from his wife's words. He blamed his wife to justify his negative feelings about the event, which doesn't serve the situation—or his relationship—very well at all. Our learned response will be based on

the objective reality that we get in touch with through *the space.*

So, what's the solution? As I've been saying, whenever an event takes place, it better serves us to have a clear and objective response to it. This happens in the fourth stage of the sequence, the *power space.* First, we need to identify the objective event, determine the biased judgment we're making of it, and see how that judgment is leading us to feel. It's at this point that we can create a change. ***The moment we become aware that our feelings are the result of our personal judgment of reality, and not the actual reality, we become capable of responding more effectively.*** Had the husband in our earlier example paused before he reacted, he would have determined that his anger was stemming from his own judgment of what his wife meant, not from what she actually said. He made this judgment because of his desperate need for worthiness and the instinctive assumption that his wife was rejecting him. Pausing and reflecting would have given him the clarity to separate the event from his personal judgment, letting him simply rewash the dish and move on.

When we get into the habit of doing this exercise repeatedly, as cumbersome as it may feel, we quickly get very good at it. Suddenly, we find ourselves much less reactive and much more secure, and we start to see a significant improvement in our relationships with others. To put this exercise to optimal use, begin by using it to reflect on past events that you already reacted to. In fact, you can do this right now. Think of an event that triggered a reaction from you, and break it down into the five stages: the objective event, your judgment of what the event meant to you, the feeling that was created by your judgment, and how you reacted. Now question the judgment you made. Is it possible you misjudged and personalized the situation, causing you to become defensive? How could your response have been different? The more you practice this exercise with past events, the easier it will be to practice it in the moment, as the event is happening.

It's important to note that the goal here isn't to change the way we instinctively react; that would only set us up to spend our lives fighting our natural reactions and feelings. Rather, the goal is to change the way we understand what happened. Once we do this, the way we react naturally changes, since we've changed one of the reasons for that reaction. You should also know that sometimes, especially when first getting started, you might get stuck in your judgment of what happened. It might feel impossible to separate your judgment from the objective event. When this happens, recruit a trusted friend to look at the situation with fresh eyes and help you see it more objectively.

Seeking an objective perspective of the events of our lives is a powerful step we can take toward looking within to access our worthiness. The *checking into reality* exercise prevents us from personalizing everything that happens to us. It allows us to slow down, notice our biases, and sidestep them before we react from a desperate and unhelpful place. We need to trust the process and stop being so sure that we know everyone else's intentions. Nothing will ever change if we continue to have the same reactions over and over again.

We must realize that when someone says something that leads us to feel something, they didn't create that feeling; we did. Did anything about the dishwashing husband's inherent value change because of his wife's comment? Did anything about his inherent value change because of the dirty dish? In his judging mind, perhaps, but not in reality. We'll spend some more time on this idea of owning our emotions in the next chapter.

Equanimity

There's a teaching from the founder of the spiritual Chassidic movement, the Baal Shem Tov, called *hishtaavut*, which in Hebrew means *equanimity*. The dictionary defines equanimity as mental calmness, composure, and evenness of temper, especially in a difficult situation. The idea of equanimity is essentially that what goes on outside of us doesn't determine what goes on within us. The greater our experience of equanimity, the better we're doing. When we seek acceptance from without, we become more and more dependent on everything and everyone around us. We become incapable of stabilizing our emotions because we place them in the hands of everything and everyone else, over which we have no control. When we live beginning within, we increase in equanimity, which results in greater peace of mind.

Most of us, if we saw someone walking another person down the street on a leash, would find it pretty strange. But metaphorically, this is happening all the time. Very often, we're the ones with the leash around our necks. But we don't see it; the leash is invisible to us. The moment we see it, we transform our lives for the better. You see, every time someone says something that gets you upset, you're essentially handing your emotions over to them and saying, "Here. Control how I feel." The people in your life who know exactly how to push your buttons might as well have a leash around your neck. But now imagine that you can keep your emotions within your control, unsusceptible to the whims of others. That's equanimity.

You might be surprised to learn that equanimity works in both directions, whether someone insults you or compliments you. When we raise our level of equanimity, we neither get upset when insulted nor jubilant when praised. In both scenarios, we assess the feedback as objectively as we can. If it has merit, we let it teach us. If it doesn't, we move on. You might be thinking, "Everyone I know gets down when someone insults them, and everyone's excitement spikes when someone praises them." This is certainly true for those who reach for the things outside themselves as a source of validation. The first time you take ownership of your own feelings and choose not to allow them to be dictated by what other people say or think, you'll realize how unbelievably liberating and powerful it is. And I want you to know that by following the process outlined in this book, you'll have that experience. Now don't get me wrong; pure equanimity is an advanced level of emotional health. But we're not here to seek perfection. We're here to make sure we're moving in the right direction, toward gaining emotional stability and fully developing ourselves.

Living in a state of equanimity doesn't mean living without emotions. We aren't robots, after all. Our emotions are a beautiful part of who we are as humans; without them, life would be a bore. Living with equanimity means having control of our emotions and choosing to respond to objective reality rather than to triggers created by our *perception* of reality. This means crying when someone dies and being joyous upon the birth of a baby; feeling happy when you see the results of your efforts, or marveling at an experience of true goodness. What I've described in this chapter isn't about shutting down your emotions. In fact, this process will help you find the courage to be in touch with your emotions like never before. One of the primary reasons that we try to control our emotions is that it takes vulnerability to asses our true feelings and express them. One more way to speak our truth is by letting those healthy emotions flow.

A Nugget of Wisdom

In the many synagogues, a large sign is placed in front of the lectern from where the cantor leads the service. On it, a verse is written from the book of Psalms. "*Shiviti Hashem lenegdi tamid.*" "I place G-d before me constantly." These words were stated by King David, whose trials and tribulations can help us begin to appreciate the magnitude of his statement. In the most trying of times, even when King David's very life was at risk, he persevered by consciously being aware of the presence of G-d. Ask yourself, "What is the meaning of placing G-d before one's self?" "How can this help me get through a very real and threatening challenge in this world?"

This is explained by the Baal Shem Tov, who reminds us that *shivisi* is an expression of *hishtavus* (equanimity). It essentially means that no matter what happens—whether people praise you or shame you—it is all the same to you. This applies to everything in your life. Whether you're eating delicacies or scraps, it's all the same to you. For when your value comes from the soul the *yetzer hara*—your self-oriented, subjective self—is entirely removed from you. When we live out of our inherent self-value, identifying with our soul, we don't personalize and subjectify our experiences. We see them not as a story about us, but rather a story for us, and we respond accordingly.

Summary

In this chapter, we discussed how important it is to simply become aware of why we act and respond in the ways we do. We then explored the powerful effect of finding the space between stimulus and response using the ***checking into reality*** exercise. Practicing this exercise repeatedly gets us in the habit of *slowing down* our response until we have more clarity, at which point we can choose a much healthier response. Next, we're going to learn a few behaviors we can improve, which will further assist our process of learning to live life beginning within. When we repeatedly engage in healthy behaviors, our emotions follow suit, and we begin to feel our inherent worthiness.

Activity

The objective of this exercise is *to help you slow down your inner processing system when you experience things in your life.* This gives you the space needed to choose how you want to feel about the situation, instead of falling into an instinctive reaction.

- Choose an event or interaction that triggered a negative emotion or response.
- Describe your judgment of the event.
- Describe your immediate feeling about the event.
- Describe your feeling after giving yourself some space to reassess the event.
- Describe your response to the event with the perspective you've gained.
- Then, after going through the previous steps, verbalize your response to the event to yourself, forging it into a true reality.

Here Are Some Examples

Example 1:

Event: My spouse told me I'm eating too much.

Judgment: My spouse treats me like a child who can't determine how much to eat on my own.

Feeling: Insulted

Space: After using my space to reassess my judgment, I realize that whether or not my spouse considers me a child, I know I'm not. I know I'm worthy whether or not I choose to eat more, and whether or not my spouse approves of it. I reflect on the amount that I have eaten in regards to healthy living.

Response: I calmly choose to say, "Honey, I really do want to eat that, so I'm going to have some," or perhaps, "Honey, while I really want to eat that, I won't because I know I want to eat healthier." In either instance, I'm not being a victim of my spouse. I'm owning my decision with great responsibility.

Example 2:

Event: My employee completed the project in the manner I explicitly told them not to.

Judgment: My employee thinks that I'm a pushover and that they know better than I do.

Feeling: Anger

Space: After using my space to reassess my judgment, I realize that my judgment may not be true. Neither my employee's opinions about me nor the possibility that I'm a pushover is what matters. In either event, I'm still worthy, and my employee still has a responsibility to listen to and follow my directions.

Response: I calmly explain to my employee, "When we discussed my expectations about this project, I was clear about how it should be implemented. While I understand that you may believe you had a better way to achieve the same results, I expect that you will complete projects the way I ask for them to be completed." I'm not becoming a victim of my employee. I'm owning my decision with great responsibility and simply responding to the reality, not to any biased feelings I may have about that reality.

Example 3:

Event: My friend asks me why I'm trying to fix something, because I'm only making it worse.

Judgment: My friend thinks I'm not capable of fixing the situation.

Feeling: Hurt

Space: After using my space to reassess my judgment, I realize that my judgment may not be true. Additionally, even if my friend thinks I'm incapable, I'm still worthy. I'll do my best to honestly decide whether I'm capable or not while knowing I'm worthy either way.

Response: I might calmly say, "You're right. I'm not great at this, but I enjoy it, so I plan to work on it until I fix it," or, "I'm actually really good at fixing things. I'm sorry you don't think so," or, "You're right. I'm not good at this. Would you mind giving me a hand?" In each case, I'm not becoming a victim of my friend's statement. I'm owning my decision with great responsibility and simply responding to the reality, not any biased feelings I may have about it.

Event: Write down the event or interaction that triggered your negative emotion or response.

_____

_____

_____

_____

_____

_____

Judgment: Describe your judgment of the event.

_____

_____

_____

_____

_____

_____

Feeling: Describe your immediate feeling about the event.

_____

_____

_____

_____

_____

Space: Describe your feeling after giving yourself some space to reassess the event.

_____

_____

_____

_____

_____

_____

Chapter 5

SHOWING UP

WRITTEN BY RABBI ARYEH WEINSTEIN

*Our emotions can be either corrupted or elevated.
Human love was not created to be without
premeditated purpose.*

– MANIS FRIEDMAN

ONE WAY TO START GAINING A SENSE OF WORTHINESS from within is by practicing the art of speaking truthfully. I intentionally said *speaking truthfully instead of always speaking the truth,* because it isn't always wise to speak all our truths to everyone. Just because something is true doesn't mean we have to share it; certain things should remain private, even if they are true. However, whenever we do choose to speak, we should be mindful to do it truthfully.

Speaking truthfully is the antidote to feeling the need to hide our true selves. It involves simply showing up as we are, without trying to make ourselves look different to the outside world. I know this can be a scary thing to practice, especially when we base our self-worth on people and things outside of ourselves. Many of us believe we'll lose acceptance from others if we speak the truth—and, to some extent, this is correct. However, most people value someone they can trust. There's no better way to build trust than to show up, even when it reveals our flaws or failures. When I started deliberately speaking truthfully, without exaggeration, minimization, or hiding of any sort, it was like experiencing a miracle. It left no room for fights, accusations, or self-conflict. No justifying or proving myself—just saying it the way it is, without fearing the outcome. Now that's pure freedom!

I remember an incident in which someone told me I'd made a comment that really hurt their feelings. I could've justified my comment or determined that the person shouldn't have gotten hurt by it; but instead, I simply said, "I didn't realize my comment would hurt you. Had I known, I wouldn't have said it. I feel bad, and I apologize. Please forgive me." No hiding. No covering up. No avoiding. I came right out and took full responsibility. He walked away feeling understood, and I walked away with no weight on my shoulders.

People often ask me how I'm able to handle students asking me questions I don't know how to answer. My response is simple: "Those are the easiest questions to answer." Whenever I encounter them, I simply say "I don't know." This response doesn't diminish my value in the students' eyes; on the contrary, it adds value to everything else I say. It lets them know that when I speak, I only do so when I know what I'm talking about. Accessing our self-worth from within leads to a powerful internal transformation; as a result of it, everything around us changes as well.

Subtle Lies

Someone asks you how many years you've been at your job, and you say 10 when it's really 8; you tell your spouse you're almost home when you haven't left the office yet. These are what I call subtle lies. Why do we tell them? Because we always want to make things sound a little better than they are; we want to make ourselves sound a little better than *we* are. This is all a part of pandering to the world around us, attempting to buy others' acceptance. By getting into the habit of speaking truthfully, even when it doesn't reflect too well on us, we create a world that's less reliant on other people's approval of us. It's shocking how often most of us deliberately paint a picture to others that differs from reality. But contrary to what we tend to think, people are more likely to embrace us when we share truths that don't make us look good than when we hide to make ourselves look better.

So how do we go about speaking more truthfully? By applying the ***checking into reality*** exercise to situations we encounter in our lives, we develop a practice of choosing to speak more truthfully. This is most helpful to practice after we've already reacted defensively toward someone based on our internal judgments. By acknowledging that we reacted because of our own issues, and not because of something the other person said or did, we build tremendous trust in the relationship. We demonstrate how truthful, responsible, and trustworthy we can be.

Taking Responsibility

Going through the ***checking into reality*** exercise allows us to become the kind of person who begins from within and takes personal responsibility for ourselves. But let me be clear that taking responsibility *doesn't* mean taking the blame. There's no use or benefit in focusing on who's at fault. But there's great value in asking ourselves what we can do about the situation and how we can contribute productively to the conversation. Instead of focusing on what everyone else should have done or should be doing—both of which are out of our control—it better serves us to do what responsible people do and take control of what *we* can do.

Rabbi Yisrael Lau, former chief Rabbi of Israel, shared part of a conversation he had in 1974 with the Lubavitcher Rebbe, whom he was visiting in Brooklyn. In the middle of the conversation, the Rebbe asked him what Jews were saying those days in Israel, following the recent Yom Kippur war in 1973. Rabbi Lau informed the Rebbe that Jews were asking each other, *"Vos vet zein"*? "What will be?" The Rebbe grasped Rabbi Lau's arm, and vehemently said, *"Yiden fregen nit Vos vet zein? Zei fregen, Vos geit men ton?"* "One should not ask, 'What will be?' They should ask, 'What are we going to do?'"

The Rebbe was emphasizing that "What will be?" is the question of a powerless person, while "What are we going to do?" is a proactive step in the direction of change. When you're at war, the last thing you want to hear is your commander-in-chief wondering, "What are we going to do?" You want to know that there's a plan, direction, and strategy; you want to be assured that you're forging ahead. Wondering what will be is an act of disempowerment and resignation; wondering what can be done is an act of liberation. You see, people who live their lives beginning within don't occupy themselves by telling everyone else what they should do, because they understand that other people's actions are out of their control. Instead, they ask themselves what can be done, and then get busy doing it.

Owning Our Emotions

On the subject of taking responsibility, there's another crucial behavior with transformative potential that we need to address. Have you ever heard someone say, "You made me feel angry!" or told someone, "You always make me feel sad"? When we use these expressions and presume that someone else is responsible for our feelings, we relinquish control over ourselves. Many people truly believe that others are responsible for what they feel. They'll say things like, "When you say insulting things to me, it hurts my feelings." This implies that there's nothing they can do about their own hurt feelings. Insulting words were spoken, they feel hurt, and that's that. End of story. But what if I told you that this is completely untrue? You see, if someone who isn't very important to us says something hurtful, the words aren't likely to hurt as much. Therefore, it isn't the words that hurt, it's the meaning we attach to those words. It's the connection we have with the people in our lives that leads us to feel insulted and give up control of our own emotional experience.

When we make our self-worth contingent upon others' words and actions, we choose a path that leads to hurt and pain. At the height of true responsibility is an acknowledgment that our feelings are our own; they are not inflicted upon us by outside sources. Have you ever seen a child get their parent angry and the parent then say, "This child makes my life miserable." Though this might seem like a demeaning statement, it's actually enormously empowering for the child. When we get angry at our children, we actually encourage their behavior; we let them know they hold the reins of our emotions. If our children see that one behavior makes us happy and another gets us upset, it creates a powerful—seductive, even—feeling for them. They realize that they're in control. And who gave them that control? Who handed over the reins? We did! By allowing our children to change our emotional state, we render ourselves powerless against them. Any time we do this with anyone, we give up our ability to choose how we'd like to respond and let someone else determine how we feel.

Taking control of our own emotions is one of the most freeing experiences we can have. Think about the difficult family member who always pushes everyone's buttons to get a reaction out of them. Now imagine the next time they try to push your buttons, you take responsibility for your emotions and respond calmly. You remind yourself that difficult people say things to trigger you, and what they're saying doesn't define reality or the truth about you. After you do this a number of times with the same person, they'll actually stop trying to push your buttons, because they'll realize it's futile. In fact, by taking responsibility for your emotions, you'll have helped not only yourself but them as well. This is a perfect example of how by transforming ourselves, we transform the world around us.

A Nugget of Wisdom

G-d gave us the free will to choose. One of the unique characteristics of human beings is our ability to override our instinctive, self-oriented nature. We can do this because we were endowed with a sophisticated level of cognition. Whenever we choose to express this part of ourselves, we are expressing our humanity. When we don't use our cognition, but rather act or respond instinctively, we're expressing our animalistic selves. Our responsibility to choose pertains not only to our behavior, but also to our speech, and even our thoughts. In fact, until we take responsibility for our thoughts, we live in conflict.

Our behaviors may be proper, but our thoughts can be filled with anger and resentment. When this happens, we are misaligned. By choosing to think more objectively, we begin to take an entirely new level of responsibility for our lives. Many people have a difficult time realizing that they can take full responsibility for what they think. Rabbi Schneur Zalman of Liadi teaches in his spiritual guide, *Tanya*, that we can be in full control of our thoughts, thereby becoming more refined.

Think of your mind as a power tool you've been given to use as you see fit. From the moment you were born, this tool has been turned on, and it will remain that way until you die. This presents a challenge, because the moment you stop feeding it healthy thoughts, it will get filled by instinctive, unhealthy thoughts. The ultimate level of responsibility we have is to feed our minds as often as possible with knowledge that will allow us to grow, and to prevent it from being passively fed by the world around us.

Summary

Let's summarize what we've learned in this chapter. There are three behaviors we must be mindful of if we want to experience peace and maximize the power invested in us. The first is speaking truthfully. Meaningful relationships depend on our vulnerable willingness to show our true selves. What we discover in this process is that speaking truthfully prevents a tremendous amount of relationship drama. The second is taking responsibility in every situation we find ourselves in, knowing that it doesn't mean we're taking the blame. We must always ask ourselves, "What can I do about this?" even when we believe the other person was wrong. This prevents a lot of unnecessary anxiety. Rather than spending time on what should've happened, we focus on making the right things happen now. The third is owning our emotions. This means realizing that no one can make us feel anything; our own internal processing system is what creates our feelings. Using the *checking into reality* exercise enables us to own our emotions and relieves us of the useless emotional pain we would otherwise carry around with us.

Activity

The objective of this exercise is to help you slowly embrace the vulnerability it takes to speak truthfully. This is the key to accessing freedom in your life and releasing the toxic energy you carry around when you hide from the truth. Reflect on your day, and call to mind a particular event or interaction. Apply the five steps of the *checking into reality* exercise to this event, then verbalize your responses to yourself, turning it into reality.

Here Are Some Examples

Example 1:

I yelled at my spouse for spending a lot of money on clothing. After calming down, I applied the ***checking into reality*** exercise and took responsibility for my anger. I realized that my anger wasn't because of her spending money, it was because I'm afraid of not having enough.

Later that day, I apologized to my spouse for making it appear as though her spending made me angry. The real reason I got angry was because I got scared.

Example 2:

My friend told me he didn't like the content of the course I was teaching, and I got upset. I angrily asserted that everyone else loves it, so he must be the problem. After calming down, I applied the ***checking into reality*** exercise and took responsibility for my fit of anger. I realized that I felt inadequate and incompetent because he didn't like the course. The next time I saw him, I apologized for getting upset and thanked him for his honest feedback. I explained that I got upset because I personalized his comment instead of hearing it as valuable, objective feedback.

Example 3:

I asked my friend to lend me $1,000, and he said no. I felt hurt that my friend refused to help me when I needed him. After calming down, I applied the ***checking into reality*** exercise and took responsibility for my hurt feelings. I realized that he has the right to use his money as he wishes and isn't obligated to live up to my expectations. I was hoping that my hurt feelings would lead him to feel guilty and change his mind.

When I called him, I apologized for attempting to use my hurt feelings to manipulate him into giving me what I wanted. I felt hurt and hoped that I could use that hurt to change his mind, which was immature of me. I thanked him for answering me honestly.

As a refresher, **the checking into reality** *exercise asks you to reflect on the following:*

1. **Event:** Write down the event or interaction that triggered your negative emotion or response.

2. **Judgment:** Describe your judgment of the event.

3. **Feeling:** Describe your immediate feeling about the event.

4. **Space:** Describe your feeling after giving yourself some space to reassess the event.

5. **Response:** Describe your response to the event with the perspective you've gained.

Write down the event or interaction that triggered your negative emotion or response.

_____

_____

_____

_____

Describe your realization about the event after using the *checking into reality* exercise.

_____

_____

_____

_____

_____

_____

How did you respond in light of your realization?

_____

_____

_____

_____

_____

_____

_____

Chapter 6

CHOOSING YOUR FREEDOM

WRITTEN BY RABBI ARYEH WEINSTEIN

If you want total security, go to prison.
There you're fed, clothed, given medical care and so on.
The only thing lacking ... is freedom.

– DWIGHT D. EISENHOWER

'M GOING TO BEGIN THIS CHAPTER by getting a little biblical. But stay with me; I'm using these references to make an important point. Isn't it interesting that G-d commands the Jewish people to recall a specific historical event on a daily basis? The reason is that past events are far more than just historical; they repeat themselves in our daily lives. Why does G-d want us to remember, every single day of our lives, the day the Jewish people left Egypt? Because the journey of the Jewish people from the slavery of Egypt to the freedom of the Promised Land is the journey every single one of us is supposed to go through in our lives. This is the paradigm of the human journey. It's the path that anyone who wants to live freely must travel. Without the willingness to travel this path, we'll remain in a perpetual state of victimhood and servitude to our desires, to other people's control, and to the circumstances of life.

The human journey involves leaving the slavery of a body-oriented life for the freedom of a soul-oriented life. The body is subjective; it enslaves us in its paranoia about the self-worth it lacks. The soul is clear; it carries no bias or subjectivity and, therefore, exists freely without the burden of fear. It can be dedicated to its values without being weighed down or slowed down by external sources. This may give you a much greater appreciation for why we're given a holiday called Passover. It's actually an eight-day annual workshop intended for us to realign ourselves onto the path of living freely.

After the Jews left Egypt during their 40 years in the desert, they often complained to Moses and asked to go back. It might seem baffling that they would ever want to go back to enslavement, but, in fact, they had a very good reason for it. It's much easier to live a life that never requires you to take responsibility. When you live this way, you can always blame your captors for your misfortune. Plus, there's a certain level of safety and predictability that comes with knowing your circumstances.

When you're not moving forward in life or taking risks in order to grow, things tend to remain the same. It's the easier approach to life. This is why people often choose to remain powerless rather than take responsibility for their lives. To be free, we need to enter into undiscovered new lands and take responsibility for how we make things work. This requires far more effort. Of course, the reward is commensurate with that effort, but many people simply don't want to do it. They'll choose enslavement over doing what it takes to win their freedom.

Our constant desire to gain acceptance from those around us is our way of living in Egypt, enslaved by what other people think about us and dependent on them for our self-worth. Freedom comes when we make the courageous choice to find our worthiness from within, knowing that we're inherently valuable no matter what others think, or how we perform, or where we stand on the social ladder.

For example, many parents take it as their responsibility to tell their children what to do and how to do it. "You shouldn't wear that." "You should act this way." "That's not how you do it." While a parents' job is to teach their children, when they make every decision for them and make commands instead of suggestions, they train them to disown their lives and just follow orders. This way of thinking follows many of us into adulthood. It shows up often in our intimate partner relationships. When we're met with constant disapproval from a spouse, for example, the easiest thing to do is resign ourselves to their will. We often hear people say, "It's no use arguing. My spouse always knows better." But part of owning our lives and becoming free is sharing our light with the world. When you encounter a difference of opinion with your spouse, you can simply say, "While I know this is the way you think it should be done, this is the way I'm choosing to do it." This doesn't mean you're picking a fight; you're simply doing what you truly feel is best.

Slavery Versus Freedom

You may have heard of Natan Sharansky, a refusenik who lived in the Soviet Union and was denied a visa to leave the country. Sharansky was a strong-willed man, and the Soviets had a hard time breaking him. Whenever they tried, they sent two officials to question him so that he wouldn't develop any kind of relationship with either of them. Since both officials knew they were being watched by the other, they were careful not to do anything out of line. This is classic behavior by people in countries controlled by fear.

Once, when he was being interrogated, Sharansky repeatedly interrupted the officers, saying he wanted to share a joke with them. Finally, they paused long enough to allow him to tell it. His joke went like this: "Brezhnev, the former premier of the Soviet Union, wasn't known to be a very intelligent man. During the Cold War, in his attempt to outdo the Americans, he called in his Russian cosmonauts and told them, 'We must outdo the Americans. We're going to be the first country to send cosmonauts to the sun.' They told him, 'Don't you realize that before we even get halfway there, we'll have burned up by the heat of the sun?' Premier Brezhnev replied, 'Do you think I'm a fool and didn't think of that? We'll send you at night!'"

After Sharansky finished the joke, he began to laugh wholeheartedly. He then looked at his interrogators and said, "I'd like to ask you a question. I'm the prisoner, yet I can sit here and laugh at this joke. Meanwhile, the two of you are the free ones, yet each of you is terrified to laugh in front of the other one. So, I wonder, which of us is really the prisoner?" This is a powerful testimony to the meaning of a truly free life. If we live in constant fear of being ourselves, unsure of what others will think or say, we're far from free. Rather, we're enslaved by our own insecurities. Only after we go through the process of learning to live life *beginning within* can we become free people.

In his renowned book *Man's Search for Meaning*, psychotherapist Viktor Frankl, a holocaust survivor, shared, "We who lived in concentration camps can remember the men who walked through the huts comforting others, giving away their last piece of bread. They may have been few in number, but they offer sufficient proof that everything can be taken from a man but one thing: the last of the human freedoms—to choose one's attitude in any given set of circumstances, to choose one's own way." Perhaps the greatest gift G-d gave humanity is the freedom of choice. The intellectual ability to differentiate, discern, and thereby make choices is uniquely human. When we can learn to differentiate between the truth and our subjective view of reality, and then make choices accordingly, we live up to what G-d expects of us.

You see, as long as we remain enslaved by the world around us, we can't dedicate ourselves to our true purpose. This is one reason why the first of the Ten Commandments is, "I am G-d your G-d who took you out of Egypt." It's G-d's way of telling us that in order to be dedicated to our G-dly purpose, we must first liberate ourselves from our personal Egypt—our body's perspective, our enslavement to other things and people. We must realize the inherent worth we all have by virtue of the fact that G-d put us here. Only then can we become dedicated to the purpose for which we were created.

Acceptance

Another important tool that's necessary for living life beginning within is acceptance. This word can be misleading, so I want to clarify what I'm saying when I use it. Acceptance means to simply acknowledge what is. It means accepting that right now, things are the way they are, and that's okay. We accept things as they are, even when they're inconvenient, painful, or unjust. But why should we accept things if they aren't what we want? For one simple reason: because right now this is the reality. Not accepting reality and living in denial is only going to create more pain and suffering for ourselves. When we fail to accept, we're in denial of reality; and from that place, we can do nothing to change things for a better future.

Acceptance isn't resigning, giving up, or giving in. It's being okay with what is, simply because it is. At the same time, acceptance can include a clear commitment to changing what will be in the future. The truth is, we can only truly change something after we've accepted it. Once we acknowledge what is, we can ask ourselves what we want to do about it. As long as we're in resistance to what's in front of us, we prevent ourselves from moving forward.

Many of the unhelpful ways we respond to the situations in our lives stem from an unwillingness to accept what is. We become less disappointed and angry when we move closer to reality and embrace what is, even if it's painful. This helps us respond more effectively, diminishing our suffering and permitting us to forgive. With every event that happens in life, we have the choice to respond in one of three ways:

1. Don't accept it and get angry about what is, but do nothing to change our circumstances.

2. Accept what is, and do nothing to change it.

3. Accept what is, and do something to change it.

Let's say you're unhappy at your job because your boss treats you disrespectfully. You've got three choices:

1. You can do what most people do, which is get angry every day, protesting about your terrible misfortune and failing to accept it as it is. This kind of response is common for those who are beginning without. If you're comfortable being powerless and prefer complaining over taking action, this is the response you'll implicitly choose.

2. You can accept the situation and choose to be happy, in spite of your nasty boss. You can remind yourself that neither your boss nor your circumstances can cause you to feel a certain way, as your emotional state is your choice.

3. You can accept what is and choose to do something about it, such as respectfully speaking up to your boss, quitting the job, or exploring a wide range of alternative possibilities.

There's a fundamental Jewish belief known as divine providence, which basically means that everything happens to us because G-d is orchestrating it. What we choose to do about the events of our lives is up to us, but they occur in the first place because of G-d. Though this concept can be difficult to grasp, it's actually the solution to many of our problems. It allows us to rest in the knowledge that G-d puts events and circumstances on our path, and it's up to us to make the right choices and learn from the challenges. The more challenging something is, the more opportunities we get to make better choices for ourselves. For me, the practice of divine providence is simply a practice of acceptance. It's a conscious shift from the perspective that life happens *to* us to the realization that life happens *for* us. Once we understand this, our anger about unpleasant situations can subside, leaving room for us to think clearly and make better decisions.

I'm going to delve deeper into an area I don't quite have the right to discuss since, thank G-d, it's beyond the realm of my experience. So I'll borrow from the words of my senior colleague, Rabbi Yisroel Deren, a highly developed individual who lost four of his eight children to Bloom syndrome. After losing his fourth adult child to this disease, he said the following to a friend of mine: "There is a phrase that some people say when they feel that life is not fair. And that is, 'Why is G-d picking on me?' Yet, if you remove one word from that phrase, it changes everything. That word is 'on.' So instead of asking 'Why is G-d picking on me,' you ask, 'Why is G-d picking me?'"

What Rabbi Deren presented is a small shift in perspective that changes everything. Instead of viewing life's challenges as unfair and insurmountable, we begin to accept them even though we may never understand them. Once we do accept them, it creates the space for us to say to ourselves, "If G-d picked me for some particular challenge, I must be up to the challenge, and I can overcome it—perhaps even with some grace."

It's only natural to get upset and angry, especially when you lose a loved one. It can feel like your heart's been ripped out of your chest. But after some time passes and the mourning has taken place, you have a choice to accept what is, forgive, and move forward. You have the opportunity to remember your greater purpose and use your pain and loss in transformative ways. Acceptance isn't about forgetting and avoiding feeling; it's about acknowledging the pain, knowing it's a part of life. It's about asking yourself, "Now, what am I going to do with this?" "How can I move forward and learn from this experience? What can I teach others about what I've learned?"

Signs That We're Enslaved

There are some common unhealthy behaviors and emotions that tend to come from a perspective of beginning without, which serve as indicators of our functioning. Once we understand them, we can use them to let us know we're looking at a situation from a biased and unhelpful perspective. Unhealthy behaviors are a sign that we need to do the *checking into reality* exercise or speak with a mentor or professional who can offer an objective perspective to help realign us. You see, even our unhealthy behaviors and emotions can ultimately serve us if we further explore them.

Anger

Let's talk about one of the most common emotions: anger. Anger shows up in different ways to varying degrees. It can appear as disappointment, frustration, or even rage, but in all its forms, it's an indication that we aren't accepting what is. When we're angry, we're essentially trying to force things to be the way we want them to be. We're using emotional intimidation to get things to go our way. It's also a desperate way to make something about ourselves, even if it's really about something or someone else. When we act out of anger, we can be quite destructive; and if it's something we do regularly, it reinforces a sense of powerlessness in our lives.

Some people believe their anger is what fuels many of their accomplishments. In other words, they confuse anger with passion. When we're passionate, we're focused on what needs to be done; when we're angry, we focus only on ourselves. Anger can lead us to be destructive toward ourselves and those around us. To begin to minimize this destruction, we must remember to tell ourselves this simple truth: "When I'm angry, I'm wrong." This is why Maimonides wrote that we should stay as far away from anger as possible. When we truly ingrain the belief of divine providence into our perspective, we reduce our anger significantly. We begin to accept the things that happen to us in life, and we stop protesting.

If someone cheated you out of $500, there's a good chance you'd be pretty angry at them. If, on the other hand, that person cheated someone else out of $500, you'd probably be much less angry. The reason is simple: When something happens to you directly, it's a personal experience, and anger then becomes a reaction you use to protect yourself. When something happens to someone else, it's no longer personal to you, so the reaction of anger no longer makes as much sense. When we stop responding to things through the filter of our subjective self, we no longer need to get so angry that we create destruction around us.

Picture this scenario: a team of commandos is rappelling from a helicopter into the middle of an enemy town full of terrorists. They need to break into a home and capture a terrorist. This mission involves navigating through many unknown variables in a very dangerous environment. Anything can go wrong at any moment. If something unexpected happens during the mission, do you think it would be wise for the commandos to get angry? Of course not! They have to remain sharp and clearheaded through-out the mission. This is obvious to most of us within the context of a scenario like this one, but we rarely apply it to our own lives. When we get angry, we say and do things that aren't so helpful to us or the people around us. Why? Because we've lost our clarity and have personalized the issue we're encountering. We become hyper-focused on ourselves and lose sight of the reality around us.

When my child gets out of bed for the third time in the middle of the night and I get angry, I must ask myself why I'm reacting this way. The event is that my child is leaving his bed and interrupting what I'm doing. My judgment is that my child is taking away my peace and relaxation. My feeling is anger. My reaction is to yell at my child. Perhaps, without realizing it, I'm trying to force my child to stay in bed by filling him with fear through my anger. Who am I thinking about? Myself. If I were thinking about my child, I would calmly ask him, "Why are you out of bed again when I told you not to come out?" If he expressed a legitimate reason, I'd respond directly to that and deal with the situation at hand. If he gave an unacceptable answer, I'd tell him to get back into bed and perhaps attach a consequence to his coming out again. That's dealing with the reality at hand in a clear-headed and straightforward way, instead of getting lost in my own reality and spiraling into anger.

Judgment

There's a big difference between making an observation and making a judgment; it's actually the same as the difference between being passionate and being angry. When I make an observation, I simply see the facts as they are. When I make a judgment, I create my own interpretation of the facts. We strengthen our innate tendency to judge when we live life beginning without. When we're in judgment, we always see external circumstances or other people as the problem. We make assumptions about other people's intentions and experiences, usually casting them in an unfavorable light.

Once we let go of the need to assign blame, we're able to stop judging. We can then simply look at the facts and ask, "What's my responsibility in this situation?" Reaching such a point is extremely powerful for ourselves and everyone around us. Once we stop judging, we can begin to unconditionally love and accept ourselves and others. When I observe other people, I repeatedly find myself standing in judgment of them. I have learned that when I remind myself to simply observe what they're doing without defining them by what they've done, I'm being fairer to them. I've also come to realize that my judgment comes from my own self-oriented need to prove to myself that I'm better than others and above certain situations. The moment I remind myself that I don't need to prove myself, I can easily observe others without needing to judge them.

Guilt

Guilt is another emotional indicator that we're sensitive to our wrongdoings. Often, we feel good about feeling guilty, seeing it as confirmation of our moral conscience. But, in fact, guilt prevents us from being productive and moving forward. To be clear, when I refer to *guilt*, I'm talking about becoming overly identified with something we've done, allowing our actions to define us. In other words, judging ourselves instead of observing ourselves. For example, guilt might lead us to say something like, "I'm such a bad person because of what I did." But when we speak to ourselves this way, we're making our wrongdoing all about ourselves and not about the issue at hand.

Guilt also makes us believe we're taking responsibility for what we've done wrong, simply because we're feeling bad about ourselves. But what this feeling of guilt actually does is keep us in a negative emotional state, leaving us little energy to take the courageous steps necessary to fix what we've done wrong. When we can accept that as imperfect human beings, we make mistakes—some of which may be serious and have significant implications—we can move forward. We can be honest with ourselves about the bad decision we've made, without condemning ourselves for it. We can ask ourselves how we can fix the damage and make things better in the future. But to do all of this, we must remain focused on the matter at hand and not get lost in ourselves.

A Nugget of Wisdom

In the very first law of the Code of Jewish Law, we're told something that isn't a law at all, but rather an instruction on developing human character. The reason this instruction is included in the very first law of the vast Code of Jewish Law is that if we don't follow it, we won't have the character to heed all subsequent laws.

The instruction states, "Do not be ashamed before those who laugh at you." If we want to choose to live based on a particular set of values, we must first free ourselves from the need to be accepted by others. Until we take ownership over our lives and stop letting others dictate our feelings and actions, we remain enslaved by them, unable to align with our values or serve G-d. In fact, G-d himself said, when taking us out of Egypt, that He must free us from our external servitude so we can have the freedom to serve our mission and our purpose.

Summary

True freedom comes with having the right to live as we believe. It involves finding the inner strength to take on the responsibilities our values demand of us. As long as we remain powerless to the people and circumstances around us, it's impossible for us to experience freedom. We're so busy trying to accommodate the expectations of the people around us—whom we depend on—that we forget about dedicating ourselves to our values. That's why it's so valuable to learn how to accept our circumstances and the people in our lives. As long as we're resisting them, we're living in denial; and in this place, we're in no position to respond.

In this chapter, we discussed the journey from living an enslaved life to living a free life. Freedom must come through our own efforts to live beginning within. Free people learn the power of acceptance. They accept reality for what it is and always ask what they can do to make it better for the future. We can't move forward in our lives unless we've accepted what is. It's for this reason that anger, judgment, and guilt always serve to indicate that we're rejecting reality and dealing with things in a way that doesn't serve us or anyone else.

Activity

The objective of this exercise is *to stop resisting reality and start accepting what is.* Only by accepting the reality in front of us can we constructively assess what we're able to do about it. Identify one circumstance or person that normally frustrates you. Make the choice to accept this circumstance or person as is, without frustration or judgment. In the same way you would notice a butterfly flying past you, fully allow this circumstance or person to be part of your current reality.

Here Are Some Examples:

Example 1:

My spouse misplaced her credit card again. I remind myself that she's naturally disorganized, and while it's easy for me to always know where my things are, it's not her strong suit. This helps me stay clear and avoid getting drawn into an emotional state. I ask myself, "What can I do to help her?"

Example 2:

I woke up with a bad cold while on vacation. Instead of being frustrated all day by my misfortune, I simply accept that I have a cold. I then ask myself what would be the most productive way to respond to this new circumstance.

Example 3:

My son needs to spend a few days in the hospital because he has pneumonia. Instead of being scared and frustrated, I simply accept that my child is very sick and needs to be in the hospital. I ask myself, "What's the best thing I can do to make it easier for my son while also managing the other areas of my life?"

Describe a circumstance or person that normally frustrates you.

_____

_____

_____

_____

_____

What do you accept about this circumstance or person that frees you from your frustration or judgment?

_____

_____

_____

_____

_____

Chapter 7

YOUR INFLUENTIAL POWER

WRITTEN BY RABBI ARYEH WEINSTEIN

We don't see things as they are; we see them as we are.

– ANAÏS NIN

B Y NOW YOU MIGHT BE THINKING, "Okay, so I see how important it is for me to take responsibility for my behaviors. But what about the people around me? How am I supposed to respond to their unhealthy behaviors, especially when I'm affected by them?" It's a natural instinct to try to help other people and get them to change. Most of us are familiar with couples who have been married for many years and still try to change each other. Though they haven't given up on each other over the years, they've made no headway. We can all relate to this on some level. We get trapped in the belief that others have to change or, alternatively, in the belief that we need to accept things about others that we can't stand. We'd rather change others than accept reality or change ourselves.

Here's what we need to know about changing others:

1. *We never change others, because it's impossible.*
   Sure, we can force others to change or place ultimatums on them, but this doesn't create *true* change. Forced

change only lasts as long as the force is applied. As we've been learning, real change only happens when it comes from *within*.

2. ***We can influence others.*** The difference between influence and forced change is the same as the difference between beginning within and beginning without. Forced change gives immediate, yet short-lived results. Influence, on the other hand, takes time but offers long-lasting results.

3. ***Influencing others begins with being an example of what we expect from them.*** It begins with changing ourselves. Working on ourselves is the best thing we can do for others.

The more committed we are to beginning within, the more capable we are of productively discussing change in others. Instead of approaching the conversation in a biased way with only our personal agenda in mind, we can thoughtfully consider the other person's perspective. When giving feedback to others, people often say, "I'm only saying this for your own good." But, for good reason, the recipient of the feedback tends not to believe it. Imposing our biases and judgments on others doesn't make them feel open to change; it usually does the opposite. When we begin within, people feel our genuine acceptance of them and become receptive to what we share.

In his book *Bringing Heaven Down to Earth Vol. II,* Rabbi Tzvi Freeman sums up the essence of what it means to begin within before asking others to change: "If you love yourself for your achievements, your current assets, the way you do things and handle the world—and despise yourself for failure in the same—it follows that your relationship with another will also be transient and superficial. To achieve deep and lasting love of another person, you need to first experience the depth within yourself—an inner core that doesn't change with time or events. If it is the true essence, it is an essence shared by the other person as well, and deep love becomes unavoidable." The first and most important thing we can do to influence others is to make sure we're living by example, simply by being anchored within.

Why People Don't Listen

Taking responsibility for our lives means taking responsibility for how we attempt to influence others. Leviticus Chapter 19, Verse 17 offers a teaching that speaks to the heart of this idea, as well as to the power of relationships in general.

> *Do not hate your brother in your heart;*
> *you shall surely reprimand your fellow;*
> *do not bear sin on him.*

The first point is essential: "Do not hate your brother in your heart." If you want to point out a flaw in someone else, first make sure you don't hate that person. This is another way of saying that you must begin within. If you unconditionally accept and love the other person, you have the leverage to point out their flaws. Unresolved issues or judgments you hold about that person—even those so subtle that you're consciously unaware of them—will diminish your ability to effectively talk to them.

Once you pass this first stage, the Torah says, "You shall surely reprimand your fellow." At this point, you're commanded to reprimand your fellow, because you've become a transparent influencer who can speak to another person entirely about them, without bringing your own issues into the conversation. Most of us have had countless experiences with pointing something out to someone—our spouses or children, most commonly—and having it fall on deaf ears. Typically, we place blame on the other person for not listening to us. But the Torah firmly reminds us, "Do not bear sin on him." This means that when someone doesn't listen to us, it's not their wrongdoing, it's ours. In the words of the great Jewish leader, the Lubavitcher Rebbe, "You are certainly the one responsible, for yours were not words coming from the heart." In other words, the first indication that we still harbor some form of judgment is that the other person isn't listening to what we have to say. People don't listen to anyone whose anger, judgment, or self-interest they feel. So, if we want to be heard, we have to take responsibility for why others aren't listening.

I want to be clear that when I speak of the other person listening to our reprimand, I mean just that, them receiving our feedback with an open mind. I don't mean them necessarily following through and doing what we tell them. The people we're addressing may choose not to follow our suggestions, but as long as we're approaching them openly and non-judgmentally, maintaining an awareness of their inherent worthiness, they'll be open to our perspective. As we work on ourselves and live our lives from within, we find that people listen to us far more. We discover that we have greater influence over other people than ever before. We become an example for others, who want to model what they see in us.

Yes, we have an obligation to bring other people's wrongdo-ings to their attention, but there's a more important obligation we need to meet first: We must make sure we've done our own work, on ourselves, in order to effectively help others. If we don't, our suggestions will backfire on us and become counterproductive. Now that we've begun to own our role in our relationships with others, let's develop a healthy perspective of others' flaws.

Flaws in Others

It's often the case that the only way we can recognize our own flaws is by seeing them in someone else. I've often had the experience of saying to myself, "Wow! So that's what I look like when I act that way." Seeing our unhealthy behaviors enacted by others often helps us get in touch with ourselves. The ability to observe and reflect on what we have seen is a huge blessing. One way to practice this is if you observe a politician who acts out of self-interest and says or does whatever serves them best. Most of us get infuriated by this kind of thing. But instead of letting it anger us, we can practice looking at their behaviors and asking ourselves, "Are my actions any better than this person's? How much of *my* life is run by self-interest?" The best way for us to respond to this is by seeing the ugliness that lives in our own lives and removing as much of it as possible. This way we can begin ridding the world of the problems that we see. We can continue to point fingers at politicians, as we so often do, but—in my observation, at least—it won't do much to help. A far more productive response is to begin within, focusing on what we can influence, which is ourselves.

We have a responsibility to help others in need. This is especially true, and especially difficult when someone hurts us or hurls insults at us. When this happens, it's important to remain focused on what's going on with that person, instead of focusing on ourselves. It helps to remember that they're suffering from a lack of self-worth and need, more than anything, to know that they're worthy. Under such circumstances, it's essential to realize that we can offer the person a special gift: affirmation that we accept and love them, even in the face of what they've just said or done to us.

Events like these present us with an enormous opportunity to take our relationships to another level. It's the only time we can truly demonstrate that we unconditionally love the person. Even though they've just done something that violates our relationship, we can choose to show them that we won't let anything break our bond, because our acceptance is unwavering. When we stop personalizing the events of our lives, we can look at them with clarity and objectivity, freeing ourselves to be present for what's going on with the person in front of us. When we practice this, we become so powerful that we can remain totally focused, even while being insulted. This gives us the ability to heal ourselves and extend sincere compassion to their true hurt, knowing that they're drowning and in need of worthiness. Then, instead of the insult turning into a fight that lasts for days or weeks, we can resolve it on the spot.

Whenever we see others' flaws or weaknesses, we're being given an enormous opportunity: to show them unconditional love. When someone behaves as we would like them to, it makes sense for us to love them. But love is only unconditional when we demonstrate it to someone who behaves in ways we don't like. This is very powerful. When my son breaks a dish, I have a vital opportunity to show him that I love him, and that he's far more important to me than a piece of China. I can always teach him to be more careful; in the moment, though, what's most important is that I hug him and say, "I love you, and I think you're just as wonderful as I did before you dropped the dish."

To be clear, I'm not suggesting we should overlook other people's wrongdoings. I'm saying that when we're healthy, we can hold them accountable while still hearing them out from a place of acceptance. We need to remember that holding someone accountable isn't synonymous with judging their self-worth and being angry at them. Let's use an example of my child talking disrespectfully to me. When he does this, he's probably frustrated or angry, which is an indication that he's drowning. His disrespectful behavior is unacceptable. However, if I only deal with the disrespect and ignore the core issue, I won't solve his problem. If I hug him and tell him I love him, even while he's disrespecting me, and then calmly tell him he needs to stay in his room for 15 minutes as a consequence of his disrespectful talk, I've been an exemplary parent.

The only way we can have the presence of mind to do this while being disrespected is by committing ourselves to living beginning within. Then we won't personalize others' comments and react from emotion. Beginning within allows us to be there for others when they need to know they're worthy, and, for those of us with children, to educate them through discipline without getting angry.

Have you ever seen a parent respond to a child throwing a fit by wrapping the child in their arms and repeatedly telling them how much they love them? It's rare to see a parent respond so brilliantly. When someone's in a state of anger, judgment, or any other form of imbalance, they're announcing to the world, "I'm insecure. I feel unworthy and unaccepted." We need to learn to see past people's actions and words to the core of what they're really saying.

Here's a simple visualization that can transform the way you respond to negativity being spewed at by someone around you. As I've said before, imagine that the person who's acting out in an unhealthy way is literally drowning in a pool of water. This will help you remain focused on their desperation and act immediately and accordingly. You see, as long as we get caught up in their craziness and begin defending ourselves against what they say, we aren't seeing clearly. We're letting our own bias and defensiveness create a false impression of what's happening. This renders us unable to be there for them and demonstrate healthy behavior because our own fear of unworthiness keeps us desperately defending ourselves.

My good friend Dr. Richard Leedes once explained this to me by using the analogy of a whirlwind. Many unhealthy people thrive by creating whirlwinds, with the intention of drawing everyone around them into it. This is very common among people who are addicted to drama. Drama is essentially a whirlwind. The key to always remember when someone creates a whirlwind is to avoid getting caught up in it. Stand at its periphery and observe it, but don't get drawn into it. The only way we can possibly help others with their destructive behavior is if we've first helped ourselves with our own flaws. Once we're clear and of sound mind, we can respond objectively to any unhealthy situation, providing the other person with what they're really seeking. This is why beginning within not only helps us, but every relationship in our lives. This is the heart of true power!

Space for Others

One of the hardest things for us to do is make space for another person. Making space for another essentially means letting the conversation be about them, too. But we can only do this when we're secure, feel worthy, and aren't dependent on others to feel good about ourselves. The greatest gift we can give to any other human being is the space for them to be themselves without judgment. In order to do this, we need to learn how to listen—not just with our ears, but with our hearts. I often have large gatherings around my Shabbat table, of 40 people or more. Typically, I pose a question and we go around the table so everyone can answer. It's quite common for someone to give a truthful answer that's unconventional or out of alignment with the values of other people around the table. On occasion, another guest will protest the respondent's answer, questioning their beliefs. When this happens, I remind everyone that we haven't come together to fact-find or fault-find. We've gathered to give people the space to be heard, and to unconditionally accept what everyone shares, no matter how we might personally feel about it.

The reality is that many people don't have a single person in the world who will make space for them to be as they are at any given moment. That's because many people live from without and, therefore, feel too insecure to create space for anyone else. Someone may have parents, a spouse, siblings and good friends, yet none of them are healthy enough to be fully there for them. So, what can be done about this? Well, you've probably figured it out by now: We begin within. We stop insisting that others change and instead become the change we want to see in the world around us. We implement everything we've learned until we become healthy enough to make space for others. As we do that, we model healthier behaviors that bring others closer to healthy behaviors of their own.

Someone once asked the Lubavitcher Rebbe, "Rebbe, what exactly do you do? And why are you admired by so many?" "I try to be a good friend," the Rebbe replied. Incredulous, the man blurted out, "A friend? That's all you do?!" Unfazed, the Rebbe responded with a question of his own: "How many friends do you have?" "I have many," the man retorted, to which the Rebbe replied: "Let me define a friend to you, and then tell me how many friends you have. A friend is someone you can think aloud to without worrying about being taken advantage of or being rejected. A friend is someone who suffers with you when you are in pain and rejoices in your joy. A friend is someone who looks out for you and always has your best interests in mind. In fact, a true friend is like an extension of yourself." Then, with a smile on his face, the Rebbe asked, "Now, how many friends like that do you have?"

A Nugget of Wisdom

One of the most well-known, as well as challenging, commandments in the Torah is "Love your fellow as yourself." Clearly, our ability to love others depends on our ability to love ourselves. When we view ourselves positively and have a healthy relationship with ourselves, we're able to have fulfilling relationships with others. On the other hand, when we have trouble accepting ourselves and constantly act out of a sense of guilt or unworthiness, we view others this way, too. People who are forgiving of themselves forgive others. People who are accepting of themselves, despite their flaws, accept others. People who live their lives believing that tomorrow will be better than today give others the space to do the same. This commandment once again reminds us that we must always begin *within*.

You can love another as much as you love yourself. Get rid of the judgment, get rid of the guilt. Remind yourself that you were created imperfect. Your job isn't to be perfect; you never will be. Your job is to do better tomorrow than you've done today. As you recognize this, something magical will happen to those around you: they'll begin to act very differently. Why? Because you've become different and, in doing so, have created a space of acceptance for yourself that others can step into as well. When this happens, you'll know you've begun fulfilling the commandment to love your fellow as yourself.

Summary

When you internalize everything in this chapter, you'll start to see how much more capable you are of loving another as yourself. As I mentioned earlier, we can't reach any depths with others that we haven't reached within ourselves. The more we accept and love ourselves, the more we can accept and love others. When we begin to be fully present for others, even in their moments of weakness, we realize the power we've attained. And we recognize that we can bring this power to others and make this world a much better place.

Activity

The objective of this exercise is to learn *to stay focused on another person's needs, even when they're attacking or accusing you of something.* When someone is behaving inappropriately, imagine that the person is literally drowning in a pool of water. This will help you remain focused on their desperation for worthiness and act immediately to assist them non-defensively, rather than focusing on your own hurt.

HERE ARE SOME EXAMPLES

Example 1:

Your boss yells at you for a mistake he made. You remain clear and don't get drawn into his drama by visualizing him drowning in his fear of worthlessness. This allows you to address his real concern and reassure him rather than become defensive.

Example 2:

Your daughter comes home upset about a low grade she received on a test. Instead of adding to her frustration, you recognize that she is drowning in a fear of worthlessness. You realize that she sees her grades as the only measure of her worth. Seeking to reassure her, you give her a hug while telling her that nothing will make you love her less, not even a low grade on a test.

Example 3:

You point out a friend's offensive behavior, and he refuses to take responsibility for his actions. Instead, he behaves like a victim, saying, "I always do the wrong thing. I always offend people." Rather than becoming frustrated by his unwillingness to take responsibility for himself, you recognize that he is drowning in a fear of worthlessness. You also see that he's in no position to take responsibility. You reaffirm your friendship with him and let him know you love him all the same.

Describe the inappropriate or offensive behavior directed towards you.

_____

_____

_____

Envision the person responsible for the behavior drowning from fear of worthlessness.

_____

_____

_____

What's one thing you can do to enhance the other person's sense of worthiness?

_____

_____

_____

_____

Chapter 8

THE BENEFITS OF DELAYING GRATIFICATION

WRITTEN BY ILENE S. COHEN, PH.D.

THE ROAD NOT TAKEN

Two roads diverged in a yellow wood,
And sorry I could not travel both
And be one traveler, long I stood
And looked down one as far as I could
To where it bent in the undergrowth;

Then took the other, as just as fair,
And having perhaps the better claim,
Because it was grassy and wanted wear;
Though as for that the passing there
Had worn them really about the same,

And both that morning equally lay
In leaves no step had trodden black.
Oh, I kept the first for another day!
Yet knowing how way leads on to way,
I doubted if I should ever come back.

I shall be telling this with a sigh
Somewhere ages and ages hence:
Two roads diverged in a wood, and I—
I took the one less traveled by,
And that has made all the difference.

– Robert Frost

There are two paths we can take in any given situation: one is the path of avoiding pain in the moment, and the other is the more difficult path of delaying pleasure for a bigger purpose. So, take a moment and ask yourself, **"Am I avoiding pain or living with purpose?"** Our cultural norms encourage us to seek Band-Aid solutions and temporary comforts—basically, whatever it takes to ease our discomfort now. This is apparent in the prevalence of casinos, commercials for psychiatric medications, and get-rich-quick schemes. Some people don't see the value in having patience during difficult times or working toward a goal; they want to lose the weight now and would rather buy the latest, greatest cell phone than save for retirement. We often make our life choices according to how we can avoid pain in the moment and, in doing so, fail to see that the path of delayed gratification is sometimes where the real solutions to our problems lie.

There's a term in Freudian psychoanalysis known as the *pleasure principle,* which is the instinctual seeking of pleasure and avoidance of pain in order to satisfy biological and psychological needs. According to Freud, the pleasure principle is the driving force guiding the id, the most basic part of ourselves. Freud compared the pleasure principle to the concept of the *reality principle,* which explains the ability to delay gratification when a situation doesn't yield immediate rewards. Whether it's saving for that future dream house, choosing a healthy lifestyle to stay healthy as you age, or putting up with a difficult job to help boost your career in the long-term, delayed gratification can yield tremendous returns while helping you develop a tolerance for waiting. According to Freud, the id rules the behavior of infants and children by only satisfying the pleasure principle; there's no thinking ahead for the greater purpose. Children seek immediate gratification, aiming to satisfy cravings such as hunger and thirst, and seeking whatever they want in the moment to ease their discomfort.

Pleasure is central to our survival. We need things like food, water, and intimacy in order to survive and pass our genetic material on to the next generation. However, as we get older and mature, we must learn to tolerate the discomfort of delayed gratification if we have a greater purpose or goal in mind. Unlike infants and young children, adults are characterized by their ability to delay gratification and tolerate hard work, discipline, and occasional unpleasantness in order to fulfill responsibilities and achieve goals. In particular, adults who begin within don't expect others to meet their needs. They understand and accept that they won't always be gratified. They also understand that their pleasure should always be aligned with their purpose.

Regardless of what our developmental stages dictate, most adults have a complicated relationship with pleasure. We spend considerable time and money pursuing pleasure now instead of delaying gratification for a greater reward or higher value later. It's complicated, because certain types of pleasure are accorded special status, such as wearing the latest fashion or driving a limited-edition car. Some of our most important rituals—such as praying, listening to music, dancing, and meditating—produce a kind of transcendent pleasure that's become part of our culture. In this way, feeling good in the immediate term isn't such a bad thing. It's provided us with an opportunity to survive and experience some relief from our stress. Most significantly, it is helping us achieve our purpose. Ultimately, pleasure for pleasure's sake is an indulgence that doesn't serve us; but when sought for the sake of a higher value, pleasure can be both meaningful and productive.

What happens when you want to be instantly satisfied in all areas of your life? What happens when you only avoid pain? What results from needing to have the newest and most expensive car, even though you're in horrible credit card debt? Living for a purpose becomes impossible at that point, because a life spent avoiding pain doesn't result in goals getting accomplished. It might be easier at first, but it won't necessarily lead to a better life in the long run. When we live in pursuit of immediate pleasure—needing to have the newest gadget the moment it's available, or wanting the perfect job without getting an education or working our way up from the bottom—we become just like toddlers again, completely incapable of delaying gratification. We set ourselves up to live from without.

Studies show that delayed gratification is one of the most effective personal traits of successful people. People who learn how to manage their need to be satisfied in the moment thrive more in their careers, relationships, health, and finances than people who give in to it. Being able to delay satisfaction isn't the easiest skill to acquire. It involves feeling dissatisfied, which is why it seems impossible for people who haven't learned to control their impulses. Choosing to have something now might feel good, but making the effort to have discipline and manage your impulses can result in bigger or better rewards in the future. Over time, delaying gratification will improve your self-control and ultimately help you achieve your long-term goals faster.

A well-known study conducted at Stanford University in the 1960s explains a lot about why it's beneficial to delay gratification. In the study, children were placed in a room with one marshmallow on a plate. The lead researcher gave the children an easy instruction: You can eat the marshmallow now, or wait 15 minutes and receive two marshmallows. The researchers found that the children who were able to wait for the second marshmallow without eating the first one scored higher on standardized tests, had better health, and were less likely to have behavior problems.

Consider the results of this study, and think about yourself and your actions. Are you able to wait for things you really want, even if it involves sacrificing pleasure and satisfaction now? Do you make decisions based on your life purpose or on what feels good now? Do you sometimes give up too soon? Can you think of a time when you accomplished a difficult task? How did it make you feel about yourself? What were the results of waiting? The tolerance you exhibit when waiting for something you want says a lot about you; it reveals the degree to which you're living from within. If there's something you want to buy, will you save now to pay with cash later, or pay with a credit card now and pay yourself back later? If you started school or own your own business and aren't seeing the rewards yet, will you keep going or give up when the going gets tough? Think about it: The things in life that bring us immediate gratification, like food, illicit drugs, gambling, screaming from anger, or using our credit cards don't necessarily bring out the best in us. They just ease our discomfort for the moment as we reach for things outside ourselves to feel soothed.

Delaying gratification isn't a new concept. Back in 300 BC, Aristotle saw that the reason so many people were unhappy was that they confused *pleasure for true happiness.* True happiness, according to Aristotle, is about developing habits and surrounding ourselves with people who grow our soul. This allows us to move toward our greatest potential. True happiness involves delaying pleasure, putting in the time, discipline, and patience instead of feeling good now. A life of purpose, aligned with the seeking of true happiness, creates real joy. It keeps our happiness meter pretty steady throughout our lives.

When we live from without, we choose short-term comfort to numb long-term pain. For example, most of us can agree that using fear, intimidation, and power can help us get what we want. We see such tactics being used around us all the time. These are the tactics of tyrants, dictators, and despots. Large countries with millions of people are kept under control this way. Intimidating and instilling fear in others doesn't require any particular skill. In fact, the less mature we are, the fewer tools we have to confront others, and the more readily we'll use fear to control them. When we use control in this way, we do it for two main reasons:

1. **To obtain the quickest results.** People have an instinctual reaction to fear and intimidation and tend to immediately comply. If they at first resist, more fear and intimidation will usually get them to surrender. Think about the person in your family who has the most power; it's probably the one who throws the biggest fit when they don't get their way.

2. **Because it requires the least amount of talent and thinking.** We all learn at a very young age how to intimidate and terrorize others. When people are struggling to get what they want from others, it's the simplest way to get what they want in that moment. Without even realizing it, we sometimes use control in order to get our way.

If we're honest, we can all recall moments when we've used these tactics to get instant gratification. What do you do when your partner doesn't want to do what you want? If you get angry, yell, sulk, or play victim, you're trying to force your partner to agree with you. What do you do when your child doesn't listen? Do you yell at them? Do you threaten them? Do you raise your voice? All of these are tactics to force your child to listen. This is exactly where our children learn how to control others—from the very model we've become for them. It horrifies us when we see them behaving badly, but what we don't tend to notice is that their behavior probably reflects our own.

As parents, we have an obligation to raise our children with a value system. We're responsible for responding when we see them talking disrespectfully or acting inappropriately. But how do we do this? Well, the quickest results will always come through forcing, punishing, and yelling at them; and the smaller they are, the better this works. It isn't hard to intimidate, threaten, or scare children into doing what we say they should do. And we don't need to take a parenting course to learn how to do this. It almost seems natural to react this way when they disobey. Trust me, as a parent, I understand this all too well. *However, this is what I call the shorter-longer way.* In the short run, we get the results we want very quickly; but it evolves into the much longer way over time.

Every time we use force, we create more distance between ourselves and the person we're pressuring. The moment we stop forcing the other person to do something—or they gain the ability to get away from us—we stop having control or influence over them. In the end, they wind up having no loyalty to us, to say the least. Citizens of a country led by a dictator will use the first opportunity they get to flee their country or bring down the regime. This is often the same dynamic reflected in teenage rebelliousness.

Here's a simple equation to help you remember this: Externally stimulated obedience equals internally stimulated fury. We feel deeply violated when we're forced to do things we don't want to do. We're being stripped of our human dignity every time we comply with force. Even G-d doesn't force us; he's shown us this by giving us free choice.

We must approach everything in life using the longer-shorter path. This is the path that requires more effort up front but yields far greater benefits down the road. It's like a really solid financial investment. The market has demonstrated that long-term investments are always the most profitable over time; the risk on short-term investments is much higher. When it comes to our relationships, investing long-term means taking the time to get our partner to see our point of view, without bullying them into it. When it comes to our children, it means lovingly insisting what must be done, not angrily doing so.

If taking the long-term approach is a better way of dealing with things, then why don't most people do it? Why do we commonly turn to the easiest way to get the quickest result? Well, the reason isn't very deep. We have a human tendency to look for the easy way out so we can feel good now instead of delaying gratification for a better reward later. It's that simple. We live in an age that's been coined the fast food era. We want it, and we want it now. We consider speediness a highly valuable asset; it gives us the feeling that we're most successful when we get things done quickly. But we all know that fast food is quite unhealthy. It offers us a quick way to resolve our hunger in the moment, but in the long term creates many other health issues that can ultimately shorten our lives. Healthy, nourishing, high-quality food takes time and effort to prepare. It takes longer upfront but saves us tremendous suffering down the road.

There's a story in the *Talmud* with Rabbi Yehoshua, who said, "Once a child got the better of me. I was traveling, and I met with a child at a crossroads. I asked him, 'Which way to the city?' and he answered, 'This way is short and long, and this way is long and short.' I took the 'short and long' way. I soon reached the city but found my approach obstructed by gardens and orchards. So, I retraced my steps and said to the child: 'My son, did you not tell me that this is the short way?' The child answered: 'Did I not tell you that it is also long?'"

Real change happens when we develop a long-sighted vision for our lives and realize that we pay a heavy price when we choose the shorter-longer way. Imagine a world occupied by people who take the longer-shorter way. Imagine a world of parents who think about how they can influence their children instead of forcing them. Imagine a world of teachers who ask how they can get through to their students instead of remaining in control of them. Imagine a world of marriages between people who choose to love their spouses instead of trying to reshape them.

There's no doubt about it, the longer-shorter way requires far more effort upfront, with no immediate results. But we need to learn to slow down and be less reactive and more thoughtful. We must stop acting instinctively and become far more responsive. Once we do this, we become a source of influence for those around us, instead of alienating the people closest to us. If we learn to take the longer-shorter way, we can reduce the biggest heartaches in our lives. We can form meaningful and true connections that last. So, ask yourself, this question: "Through every step of my life, am I choosing the easy way, or am I making strides on the longer-shorter path?"

Hiding Behind Lies

How much money have movie theaters and amusement parks lost on families with 13-year-old children whose parents claim to be 12 so they can pay the child rate? I suspect the amount is staggering. And this scenario gets played out in many aspects of life; in fact, it occurs among pretty honest people as well. Whenever I bring this up, people want to change the subject right away. It hits too close to home. And honestly, I have no doubt that I, too, have been dishonest in similar ways. The difference is that now I dig deeper into what

I'm doing, even if it's only a seemingly small white lie.

I'm raising this particular example because most of us have probably told similar white lies to gain some advantage or personal benefit. We often rationalize our lying with different explanations that seem to make sense to us, but are usually just juvenile justifications. And our reasoning usually holds up, since most other people use the same reasoning to explain their own behavior. What helps me step away from dishonest behavior, no matter how small it may appear, is gaining a deeper understanding of the damage my negative behavior creates in the long run.

I'm always trying to get to the bottom of what motivates our lying and what effects our lies have on us. What I've found is that when we lie, we don't show up. And hiding in this way has enormous ramifications not only in our relationships with others, but also in our ability to stay in touch with reality and with ourselves.

There's a saying in Yiddish that "a fool only fools himself." In other words, while we may be fooling others through our lies, we're the ones most blinded by them. We do everything possible to make our lies believable that eventually we begin to believe them ourselves. This is why, when we hear people using weak justifications for their actions, we have a hard time helping them realize how flimsy their reasoning is. Working with convicted felons, I saw people attempt to use justifications for even the worst of crimes. This led me to understand that when we can find a way to explain our actions that makes sense to us, we let ourselves off the hook.

There are a few things we need to pay attention to in order to see how lying helps us hide and avoid pain in the moment. When we're unwilling to show up for others, we aren't present enough to be in a relationship. When we don't show our true selves, we simply aren't there, and the relationships we have with others end up being quite shallow. Lying and hiding lead us to create a distorted view of reality. We argue that circumstances are always different from what they are, and we come to feel safer lying, hiding, and creating delusions rather than facing reality. I probably don't need to explain how unhealthy it is to live in a world of delusions. It's actually very hard to lead a productive life when our feet aren't on the ground and we're out of touch with reality.

Lying is just one of the tactics we use to provide us with short-term comfort, but very often it leads to long-term pain. This is always true whenever we try to change the reality around us, instead of taking responsibility and owning up to who we are on the inside. Showing up in life and owning who we are can be painful in the moment; we fear the reactions we're going to get from other people, and rightfully so. We've had enough experience to know that when we do share our faults or weakness with others, there's always someone who'll try to capitalize on our vulnerability. But the power of being vulnerable is in speaking truthfully, even though some may not understand us. As we do it, we discover the enormous power of just showing up—no more games, no more hiding, no more make-believe, no more false realities, no more delusions. We simply show up and share who we are as we are in this moment. When we begin doing this, we start to discover how powerful and peaceful this approach to life is. Over time, the fear fades, and people start admiring us for the enormous courage it takes to live a life of truth.

Speaking truthfully connects us to the core of our purpose in this universe. When G-d created the universe, He—though infinite and limitless—needed to step aside and make space for other existence aside from Himself; He essentially went into hiding. In fact, the way we say universe in Hebrew is *Olam*, a word derived from the word *he'elam,* which means hidden. This is because the very existence of the universe came about through G-d hiding himself. Part of our mission in this universe is to reveal G-d from within the universe, which is why living a purpose-driven life is so powerful.

Every time we hide behind a lie, we perpetuate the very problem in the universe that we're supposed to be correcting. And every time we speak truthfully, we correct the fundamental weakness of the universe. When we accept our full responsibility and realize that we're part of something much greater than ourselves, we understand that lying has much larger ramifications than whatever isolated incident we're dealing with in the moment.

With all of this in mind, I encourage you to be courageous. Take on the challenge of becoming someone who's committed to speaking truthfully, and realize that the one who gains most from this is none other than you. The next time you're faced with the opportunity to make a short-term gain by hiding behind a lie, remember the effect you're having on the greater universe, and choose the longer-shorter way.

Being Courageous

Living courageously is not about being tough or being stronger than others. It's also not about being immune to the fear of something new or seemingly dangerous. It's not about pressuring yourself to feel confident in new and unknown situations, either. It's about accepting fear and yourself as you are. Delaying gratification is all about being courageous.

Courage is the ability to do something, even if it scares us. Courage is finding the strength to face pain, anxiety, fear, and grief without looking for immediate relief. Courage is having the ability to act on our values despite the disapproval of others. Courage is doing what's uncomfortable now for a greater reward later. Having courage means moving toward fear, validating our experience, and doing what needs to be done no matter how it makes us feel. Most people think of being courageous as showing a brave face and believing that strength is our only option, but that isn't the case. Courage is all around us and, in fact, all we need to do is look into nature to find examples of it.

We can see baby birds stepping off the edge of their nests to fly because that's what chicks do—they find the courage to fly.

We can see chipmunk pups emerging from the underground sanctuary of their nest for the first time because that's what chipmunk pups do—they find the courage to pop out of their nests and run around.

We can see toddlers taking their first steps even though they may fall, or kids walking into their first day at a new school because that's what humans do—they find the courage to get up and grow up.

The modeling of courage in nature is an endless stream of purposeful and courageous action that offers lessons on the lived experience of everyday courage. It's doing the hard thing now, the thing that scares us the most, for a greater purpose later. Nature already gets this; it understands what it takes to grow and survive. It's time we find the courage to do the same. We do this by tackling each situation life hands us, even if it makes us feel like throwing up.

No Pain, No Gain

We all wish we could live a life of pleasure and bliss, free of pain, worry, or anxiety. And, of course, we tend to wish the same for our children and other loved ones. As we evolve, most of us learn that there's no escape from hardship in our own lives; but despite knowing this, we still hope that through our ability to control so much of our loved ones' lives, we can at least protect them from the many challenges we've encountered in our own lives.

The truth is, there's no way of protecting anyone from the challenges of life. What we really need to understand is that even if we could, it wouldn't benefit us or them. Why? Because without challenges, we don't develop or grow. For example, if children don't rise and fall, and rise and fall again, they never learn how to walk. To learn any subject, we must go through the discomfort of study. Only one who has gone through the effort of raising a child can experience the satisfaction of those efforts. Only through extreme dedication and hard work can a student become a doctor. Only through trial and error, which sometimes even affects other people's lives, can the doctor become even better. Only those who have suffered a loss can truly console someone experiencing the same. There are deep levels of emotional and intellectual wisdom that we only receive by going through difficult experiences.

No pain, no gain is a difficult truth we'd rather ignore. Yet it holds true. The best way to dispel darkness is with a ray of light. The best way to dispel fear is by looking it in the eye. The best way to look at a challenge is to ask, "What potential opportunity lies behind this?" We must know that G-d constructed the world in such a fashion that the opportunity always lies behind the challenge, and the pain always comes before the gain. For me, this book is a perfect example. I spent over a year working just to complete a first draft, and I'll probably spend much more time before reaching the results I'm trying to achieve. I know that the more time I put into it and the longer I remain dedicated to it, the greater the results will be.

If you have children, work with kids, or have them in your family and want to make them happy, practice teaching them how to respond to challenges rather than protecting them from those challenges. Challenges are one of the greatest sources of potential growth and satisfaction. The more that we protect our youth, the more difficulty they'll face when they encounter things we can't protect them from. The more we guide and encourage our kids, the more independent and capable they'll become. I don't keep my kids from cooking because they might burn themselves; I encourage them to cook while observing them from behind. I don't protect my kids from carrying a glass bowl; I encourage them to do so carefully. If the lesson costs me a $15 bowl, it's the least expensive tutor I've ever hired for a lesson that will last a lifetime. There's no greater teacher than experience. I'd never let my kids do things that would put them in real danger, and I make sure to protect them from experiences that I assess to be beyond their ability to handle. But there's a big difference between assessing real danger and limiting our children because of our own fears.

There's a story about a man watching a butterfly trying to squeeze out of a cocoon. After a few hours, the butterfly stopped moving. Feeling compassion for the poor butterfly, which seemed to be stuck, the man pulled a knife from his pocket and cut open the cocoon. The butterfly emerged very easily, but had a withered body and shriveled wings; it was unable to fly. What the man, with all his kind intentions, didn't know was that the tiny, restrictive opening in the cocoon was G-d's way of forcing fluid from the butterfly's body to its wings so that it would be healthy and fly.

There's a Jewish teaching that Rabbi Weinstein has been sharing with his children since they were very small. It's one of 12 unique Jewish teachings that they all know by heart in Hebrew. Whenever they have a family birthday, they repeat all 12 passages. One particular teaching states, "If one says I have put forth effort and did not succeed, don't believe them. If one says I have not put forth effort and have succeeded, don't believe them. If one says, I have put forth effort and succeeded, believe them." The message is very clear: Things that come without effort either aren't an achievement or don't have much meaning for us. When we put forth effort, it's impossible for nothing to be achieved. The bottom line is that we must exert effort.

This takes us to the fundamental value of living life with a long-term outlook instead of seeking short-term gain. Like I've said before, anyone who invests in the market long-term will always come out with a gain. It's those who become scared when the market drops and sell out of fear who always lose. Offering ourselves immediate comfort by taking the shortcut to avoid pain ends up costing us significantly down the road. Our shortcuts render us unprepared for life.

Rabbi Dr. Abraham Twerski shares an insight that he learned from lobsters. Lobsters are soft animals that live inside rigid shells that don't expand; yet somehow, lobsters still grow. As they get bigger, the lobsters' shells become very confining, and they begin to feel pressured and uncomfortable. So, as nature would have it, they go under rock formations to protect themselves from predatory fish, cast off their shells, and produce new ones. Eventually, the new shells become uncomfortable as the lobsters continue to grow; so once again, they discard their shells and produce larger ones, repeating this process many times throughout their lifespan.

The stimulus for a lobster's growth is its discomfort. If lobsters avoided this discomfort, they'd never grow. Then they'd never cast off their restrictive shells and be able to grow new ones that serve them better. From the lobster we can learn to realize that times of stress are opportunities for growth, and if we use adversity properly, it can help us thrive.

I leave you with this question. Next time you experience a hardship or challenge in your life, will you get distracted by your attempt to understand why it happened and protest how unfair it is, or will you focus on what you can do with the experience by noticing the opportunity for growth it's offering you?

A Nugget of Wisdom

If there is one religion that embraces intimacy between spouses, it's Judaism. When a couple is intimate, a unity is created between both people that pervades all levels of their being—spiritual, emotional, and even physical. According to the mission of revealing oneness in the universe, every act of unity is a major achievement. Intimacy between spouses is, therefore, one of the holiest acts anyone can engage in. No guilt needed!

At the same time, however, G-d gives us guidelines for when it's appropriate to be intimate, and when it's forbidden. Even this pleasurable need that G-d embedded within humanity has limitations and controls. That's because pleasure for its own sake, a form of self-indulgence, is usually self-destructive. Purpose is the key to transforming something self-indulgent into something meaningful.

Summary

People who learn how to manage their need to be satisfied in the moment thrive more in their careers, relationships, health, and finances than people who give in to it. However, when we live from without, we choose short-term comfort to numb long-term pain. Additionally, we use unhelpful behaviors like fear, intimidation, and power to get us what we want now. However, like we have been saying, this is the shorter-longer way. In the short-run, we get the results we want very quickly; but it evolves into the much longer way over time. For example, the stock market has demonstrated that whenever someone invests long term, they always make more money over time.

This takes us to the fundamental value of living life with a long-term outlook instead of seeking short-term gain. This is why we must have courage. Courage is doing what's uncomfortable now for a greater reward later. Having courage means moving toward fear, validating our experience, and doing what needs to be done no matter how it makes us feel.

Activity

The objective of this exercise is to *move away from our urge to seek comfort now in order to receive better rewards later.* During the course of your day, identify a moment when you really want to do something now that you know won't benefit you in the future. Try to focus on what your long-term goals are, instead of satisfying your desires in the moment. Your objective is to not give into your immediate need to soothe any discomfort you're having, but rather wait out your need for immediate gratification in order to understand what's better for you and your future.

Here Are Some Examples:

Example 1:
You're on a diet, because you have a goal to lose 20 pounds and maintain a healthy lifestyle. At your holiday office party, your favorite cookies are spread out on the buffet table. You decide to walk past the cookies and go to the vegetable platter instead.

Example 2:
A new pair of shoes just came out, and you love the style and fit. However, they're $200 over your budget. You have a store credit card you can put them on, but you know the interest payments will limit how much money you can put into your retirement account. So, you decide to get a less expensive pair of shoes that fit in your budget, and save a little extra money each week until you can afford the shoes you really want.

Example 3:
Your child is acting up and throwing a tantrum. You really want to yell and demand that they behave; but instead, you calm them down, lovingly embrace them, and encourage them to talk about what's really bothering them.

Identify what a short-term gain would look like versus a long-term outcome?

_____

_____

_____

_____

_____

_____

Did you self-soothe and find the courage to resist the short-term gain?

_____

_____

_____

_____

_____

_____

Did you get through the urge to feel satisfied now and feel a sense of relief that you didn't give in?

_____

_____

_____

_____

_____

_____

Chapter 9

LIVING INTENTIONALLY

WRITTEN BY ILENE S. COHEN, PH.D.

If I am I because I am I, and you are you because you are you, then I am I and you are you. But, if I am I because you are you, and you are you because I am I, then I am not I and you are not you.

— R' MENACHEM MENDEL OF KOTZK

WHEN SARA FIRST CAME TO MY OFFICE, she had a pretty good handle on what she wanted for her life and what type of person she wanted to be. She was pretty clear about her guiding principles and core beliefs; however, her actions didn't always fall in line with those beliefs, or with how she truly wanted to treat others. She'd often give in to her impulses in the moment, forgetting what was truly important to her. For example, Sara made enough money to save for a down payment on a condo, which was a lifelong dream of hers. However, she'd regularly spend all her income on what she called "nonsense" and never saved any of it. She wanted to have a healthy lifestyle and stay in shape, but she found herself overeating and making frequent appearances in the fast food line. Sara also wanted to treat her sister with more respect, but she often found herself frustrated, distant, and annoyed by her. As a result, she was usually unkind to her.

When I met her, Sara was completely frustrated with herself. She wondered why she couldn't do what she needed to do, especially since she was so clear about her goals, values, and principles. She told me she wanted to explore how she could become more intentional with her actions instead of being so impulsive. I think most of us can relate to Sara's experience of living through impulsive reactions rather than thoughtful responses. Knowing this, what can we do about it? How can we make changes? Well first, we can begin by becoming aware that it will better serve us to live an intentional life guided by our principles instead of what feels good in the moment.

Leading a lifestyle based on conscious attempts to align with our values and beliefs—in other words, living an intentional life—isn't easy. Like Sara, we often live from our impulses, automatically making decisions without considering our long-term goals or personal values. Living intentionally calls for us to move from living *on autopilot,* to living *on purpose.* The sooner we understand our worth, living from *within* and with *intention,* the better and more fulfilling our lives become. Living a good life of quality and purpose certainly requires intentionality. In the hectic, busy, and hurried world we live in, it's easy to turn off our intentions and just float through life. Our culture, which encourages selfishness and excess, makes living intentionally a particular challenge. And within the context of our society, which promotes rushing to gain more, finding satisfaction with a life that best suits our own personal values takes effort.

To live an intentional life, it helps to start by laying a foundation through the ideas presented in this book, then adding a couple of practical steps to bring out our best selves. We can't live intentionally without determining our own guiding principles or emotional states. Understanding the concept of *differentiation of self* is also critical. All of these ideas and concepts can help us learn to respond to people and situations in ways that better reflect our values and beliefs and hold us accountable to live more authentically. When we react to people and circumstance based on emotions and anxiety, we live from impulse rather than intention.

Determining Your Guiding Principles

To live from within and with intention, it's instrumental to know what values and principles guide you. So, how do you come up with your own guiding principles? Start by writing a *belief paper,* which will help you determine the driving force behind your efforts to live intentionally. You might be thinking, "If I know what I value and what's important to me, it should be pretty easy to come up with this, right?" Well, from doing this exercise with many people, I can tell you that it isn't as easy as it may seem— especially when I ask you to include in this paper what you believe, where those beliefs came from, and what they're based on.

Writing this paper might lead you to realize that some of your beliefs aren't your own. If this is the case, you'll have to dig a little deeper in order to start living based on your own values, rather than on what other people tell you to value. Once you have that down, think about what you consider non-negotiable. Consider what it takes to build principles that will help you live with more intention. In this section, you'll see me provide more questions than answers; that's because no one but you can come up with the answers for your own life. I have principles that guide my life, but I don't expect everyone to live by the same values that I do. In fact, one of my guiding principles is to not impose my beliefs and values onto other people, and to be tolerant and accepting of others' beliefs. Some questions to ask yourself to help in developing your *belief paper* are:

1. What are some principles that I strongly believe in?

2. Where did these beliefs and principles come from?

3. What theology are my values based on?

4. What do I truly value? What's important to me?

5. What beliefs, values, and, principles do I consider non-negotiable?

6. Do my actions fall in line with what I truly believe is right for my life?

Determining Your Inner Emotional State

To live with intention, it's vital to determine your own inner emotional state first. I don't have to tell you that it can be a rough world out there. So, it should come as no surprise that there are many different approaches people take to deal with the challenges that come their way. Some of us become intimidated by people who are rougher, and we back away in order to make room for them. Others do quite the opposite; they develop their own rough stance, ensuring that they don't get pushed around by others. Some of us are sensitive to certain situations, so we avoid them altogether; others develop thick skin so that those situations won't hurt or bother them. However, when we go through life reacting to our circumstances, it's impossible for us to be guided by our intentions.

When I was in my early 20s, I was very intimidated by other people. If anyone became loud, or voiced an opinion that was different from mine, I'd quickly back off. I didn't have the inner courage or knowledge of my self-worth to stand up to people who showed a strong presence and were willing to bully or intimidate me. At that time, I understood that I had only one of two choices: (1) become less sensitive by developing thicker skin and learning not to care or be concerned about the things and people around me, or (2) remain sensitive and thin-skinned, knowing that I can't step into arenas that are too rough for my sensitive personality. Though I didn't particularly like either of these choices, I truly believed they were the only ones I had.

As I got older and began to educate myself, I realized that neither being overly-sensitive nor being thick-skinned is the intentional way to deal with difficult situations or people. For example, I considered the salesman who commits himself to selling, even if he receives many rejections for every sale he makes. Not only does he get turned down numerous times, some of the rejections are harsh, insensitive, and insulting. How would you coach the salesman to remain intentional, despite the challenge of this enormous amount of rejection? Some people may tell him, "You have to develop thick skin so that the comments won't bother you. If they insult you, insult them right back. Show them you can be just as nasty as they are." Others may tell him, "Get out of sales. It's not for sensitive people like you. To be a good salesman, you need to be able to handle rejection without letting it affect you. If you're this bothered by rejection, you're in the wrong line of work." As I see it, neither of those approaches offers proper coaching for the salesman. The first one advises him to lower his standards, and the second encourages him to avoid the problem. Neither of those solutions will provide the salesman with an opportunity to act intentionally and respond in ways that better align with his core values and beliefs.

When we're sensitive, we can easily fall into avoidant or reactive behaviors, as we find ourselves susceptible to being taken advantage of by others' insensitivity. When this happens, we suddenly find ourselves compromised. We might end up feeling weak and vulnerable because of our sensitive nature. To spare ourselves this vulnerability, we move to protect ourselves and wind up reacting with the same kind of insensitive behavior we were trying to avoid in the first place. To some extent, this might serve to avoid some hurt feelings. It might lead us to draw the conclusion that if we become tougher, put up a front, or avoid our feelings altogether, we'll get hurt less. We might also decide to simply avoid people and circumstances that exploit our vulnerability. But with both of these approaches, we change ourselves to react to our circumstances in this sometimes harsh world; neither one exemplifies living from *within*.

Keeping all of this in mind, there's an intentional approach that allows us to determine our own emotional state and respond to situations without having to change our values and goals in the process. It's also a way to reveal our personal inner power. This approach won't just serve a salesman much better, it will serve all of us in living through purpose. Be warned, it's not the easiest approach; but it's the most effective and rewarding by far. First of all, it's important to remember that sensitivity is a great virtue, not a weakness. Being sensitive to others is important for our relationships; it helps us remain connected to the people around us. Now imagine there was a way to remain sensitive to others without being easily wounded by their insensitivities. Imagine you could learn not to run away and avoid problems, while also not resorting to the inappropriate behaviors others display. Well, this is possible when we learn to take full responsibility for our feelings. Once we do, we experience the power and freedom of being in control of the way others impact us.

When someone can say something hurtful to us and it doesn't ruin our day, that's when we know we're in control of how we feel. We can get so tied up in what others say and do that we lose ourselves in the process. But instead of resorting to reactivity, we can take people's hurtful words and actions less personally and change the way we respond to the hurt that may echo inside us. This is what it means to live intentionally.

The art of being able to interact with people by staying connected and managing our emotions is the mark of a person who lives with true intention. Intentional people don't live through reaction and fear merely because they're highly affected by the behaviors of the people around them. Rather, they determine their inner emotional state and how they respond to others based on their values. When we answer people from intention, maintaining our objectivity, we can see how quickly people change the way they talk to us. When we don't react to others based on our own anxiety and fears, we have a better chance of reaching them in a different way. So, how do we learn to do this? We start by choosing to answer people intentionally in every situation we encounter. When we dedicate ourselves to changing the way we function throughout the course of each day, we learn to more wisely choose our responses to the world around us.

Jennifer came to my office without really knowing what her goals were for therapy. She wasn't exactly sure what the problem was—or if there was even a problem at all—but she thought it would be a good idea to check in with a therapist and process a few things. As we got to talking, I discovered that Jennifer had been floating through life without really feeling anything. She had developed the skill of cutting off from her emotions and avoiding problems or difficult people.

Growing up with five younger siblings, Jennifer came to believe that there wasn't much room for her emotions. If she got upset about anything, she was immediately shut down by her parents, who expected her to be well-behaved all the time, bring home perfect grades, and help take care of her siblings. Although she had gotten used to disconnecting from her emotions, Jennifer considered herself to be a compassionate person. She explained that she was always accommodating her family and friends' needs. However, she admitted to me that there wasn't much feeling behind her actions; it was all pretty automatic, and she kept it that way to avoid problems. As Jennifer and I got to know each other, she became increasingly concerned about her lack of emotions, especially when her last boyfriend broke up with her because he found it hard to get to know her. During their final conversation, he told her she lacked enthusiasm for life, and he didn't believe she really cared about him.

At a young age, Jennifer learned to numb her emotions and go through life without intentions or goals for the future. Children can only experience their true feelings when there's someone there who accepts them, understands them, and supports them fully. Jennifer didn't have anyone like that in her life. In fact, she felt she would lose her family's love if she was "defiant" and showed her feelings; so, instead, she learned to swat emotions away like annoying insects. She continued to live her life numb and passion-less. As a result, she never learned how to let her emotions in and regulate them properly.

Living intentionally is so essential that its absence takes a heavy toll, typically causing us to lose our sense of self, our personal goals, and our close relationships. In order to become wholeheartedly ourselves, we must try—through an often lengthy process—to discover our own beliefs and values. And the truth is, this may create discomfort before it gives us a new sense of freedom. Jennifer would have continued on her journey in the same way she had been doing if she hadn't started to learn that acknowledging old feelings isn't deadly, but instead very liberating. Showing up and bringing her own needs into the picture wasn't a bad thing; it was something that could bring her to life.

Accommodating the needs of others often leads us to only reveal what's expected of us; this, in turn, renders us unable to differentiate our true intentions. Failing to live as a differentiated person leads to a sense of emptiness. When we can't sense our own needs, we wind up feeling alienated, even from ourselves. Jennifer came to the understanding that in order to get love and acceptance from her family, she had to repress who she was; but this came at a big cost to her emotional development. When it's only about others, there isn't any room for self. Jennifer was regulating herself for others, and she realized it was no longer working for her life or her relationships.

Jennifer came to realize that the urges, whims, and fleeting emotions she felt didn't define her. If you want to know your true intentions, don't ignore your feelings; instead, accept them as your own and allow them to connect you with your deepest values. When we ignore ourselves and our true intentions, we betray who we are and give up on what we value most. If you want to live an intentional life, you must first discover who you are by determining your inner emotional state; this is something that takes searching to discover. It never happens when you're stuck in fear or doubt, reacting to the world around you; and it certainly doesn't happen when you're disconnected from yourself. This is where the next step in living intentionally comes in: developing a higher level of differentiation of self.

Differentiation of Self

Differentiation of Self, is our ability to separate feelings and thoughts. Undifferentiated people cannot separate feelings and thoughts; when asked to think, they are consumed with feelings, and have a hard thinking logically and basing their responses on that logic. They also have difficulty separating their own feelings from other's. Differentiation is the process of freeing yourself from your family of origin in order to define yourself, this means being able to have different opinions and values than your family, but also being able to stay emotionally connected to them. It means being able to calmly reflect on a conflicted interaction afterward, realizing your own role in it, and then choosing a different response for the future.

As Jennifer's case reveals, it's hard to develop a sense of yourself and your personal intentions within an intense family. Most of us merely vanish in our relationships with family members who aren't accepting of who we are. However, people whose wellbeing and functioning depend on what others say or don't say have a low level of differentiation of self. When we live with intention, we have a far less anxious investment in others, so we don't need to hide ourselves in fear. It's important to note that *differentiation of self* isn't something we accomplish in one weekend. It exists on a spectrum from highest to lowest functioning that evolves throughout our life journey. We're born with a basic level of differentiation that's determined by our families. When we work on certain aspects of our lives, we can raise our level of differentiation, allowing us to live more intentionally.

Differentiation of self gives us the ability to be part of our environment and engage in our relationships while remaining in control of our own minds. People with a higher level of differentiation are able to: (1) think logically, even in the midst of others' emotional reactivity; (2) navigate difficult situations using their goals and values, rather than succumbing to urges to distance themselves or react with anger; and (3) be less invested in being accepted and more invested in living from within. When you move toward a higher level of differentiation, you build more of a *self,* opening up avenues to reduce your anxiety and intentionally respond to everything around you.

Once you're aware that you're fully responsible for your own emotions, you can feel and express them without being controlled by them. You can take on challenges, become aware of your part in it all, and have the ability to manage yourself through anything. Owning your own emotions helps you stay guided by what you think is best and what you're trying to achieve. This work is all about being who you want to be, which includes responding in ways that are beneficial to your health and functioning. It takes time, though, and involves lots of practice getting uncomfortable with your new responses to the world around you.

Having a high level of differentiation includes maintaining a balance between the drive to be an individual and the drive to be together with others in relationship. Our togetherness urge pushes us toward others for attachment and approval. When the togetherness is too intense, we may pull away from people too much or lose ourselves in the relationship. This is an automatic process for us, especially when we're anxious. However, as human beings who thrive on connection, it's important that we avoid disconnecting completely. Striking the balance between individuality and togetherness comes with knowing who you are and what you value, without having it determined by others. Once that's clear, you can be in relationship with other people while maintaining a sense of who you are as an individual; you can be the person you want to be while also nurturing your relationships. In other words, the core of who you are won't have to change according to who you're with at any given time.

I once worked with a client who would change the type of clothes, food, or music she liked based on the guy she was dating. She had a low level of self-worth and would create a new self to fit with whoever she was with at the time. She would give herself up so completely in her romantic relationships that she had no idea who she was when she was alone. Her relationships never worked, because they were based on her reacting to her partner, versus responding to her partner through her own voice and values. No one else can truly tell you who you are, what you value, what you like or dislike. Nobody benefits when you compromise who you are.

When you first start trying to live an intentional life, you're likely to push toward defining yourself as separate from others. You'll move toward adopting your own beliefs, values, and choices, developing a real sense of autonomy. Paradoxically, all of this will allow your relationships to truly flourish. Building a sense of self that includes personal beliefs, goals, and intentions is a difficult process. But the more intentional you become, the easier it will be for you to manage your natural, opposing impulses for autonomy and togetherness. The more you respond to others versus react to them, the more available you'll be to connect in ways you never imagined.

Human Connection

In this chapter, you've learned to start living an intentional life by determining your guiding principles, attuning to your inner emotional state, and becoming more clearly differentiated. So how does all of this play into human connection? The other chapters of this book have addressed ideas such as knowing your internal worth, changing from within, truly knowing yourself, showing up, choosing your freedom, acknowledging your influential power, and delaying gratification. In each part of the book, we attempted to maintain an emphasis on the importance of relationships, because let's face it: life isn't much without human connection. In fact, we're biologically wired to be in relationship. Think about how boring and purposeless this life would be without friendships, intimate relationships, or family. Being human comes with a desire to be loved and accepted for who we are, and to offer the same to others.

Did you know that newborn babies need to be held and embraced in order to experience healthy psychological development? Studies show that infants who experience little to no human connection and comfort fail to develop in healthy ways and, in some cases, even die. It's essential to be aware that the goal of working on ourselves isn't to become hyper-focused on only ourselves. The idea is to develop ourselves while always keeping in mind the importance of remaining connected to others. Opening ourselves up to being vulnerable and experiencing the benefits and downfalls of all types of relationships is part of remaining connected. Vulnerability is hard to express, because it involves accessing parts of yourself that others may have disapproved of in the past. That's probably why you didn't access those parts of yourself in the first place. When you develop a high level of differentiation, you'll have a better time managing your emotions when people aren't on their best behavior, because you'll be aware of and open to your own vulnerabilities. Once you become aware of all the parts of yourself, you won't feel the need to close yourself off to others. When you deeply and solidly live intentionally, your life and relationships serve as a mirror for what you truly want. It takes a lot of strength to honor all the parts of yourself, regardless of how others feel about it. But instead of avoiding the people who don't always agree with you, you can face them, stay connected to them, and maintain who you are at the same time. You can do this because you've accepted your emotions as your own, which lets you be comfortable with who you are, no matter what.

A Nugget of Wisdom

Each of us was created for a unique purpose that's completely our own. However, our individual purposes are meant to be directed toward a single common mission, making this world peaceful and unified through awareness of its creator, a global form of value from our G-dly self. On one hand, we are individual and unique; on the other hand, we are part of a common collective. This is a fine balance that each of us is meant to struggle with throughout our lives. We are all tasked with holding onto the uniqueness G- d endowed us with, actualizing it to its fullest potential, while at the same time remembering that we're all part of something far greater. Your individuality must complement and bring wholeness to the collective containing all of us. It mustn't be used as a form of isolation.

When the Tabernacle was first built in the desert, not long after the Jews left Egypt, there was an inauguration; each day was designated to one of the twelve tribes. On its particular day, the prince of each tribe brought offerings to G-d on behalf of the tribal community. Fascinatingly, each prince brought the exact same offering. You may wonder, what was the point of bringing the exact same offering that was brought yesterday and the day before? The answer is simple: Even when we do the same thing and engage in the same effort as someone else, we do it with a unique individuality that differentiates us. Every prince brought the exact same offering, yet it was done in a unique style with a special focus. Be you. Be only you. Be your piece in the cosmic puzzle so that you bring completion to the greater reality around you.

Summary

Living an intentional life isn't as easy as it may sound. Most of us live on autopilot, reacting to our circumstances instead of making decisions based on our long-term goals and values. And most of the time, we don't even realize we're living that way. If we want to live from within, we can't keep making decisions based on reactions to outside circumstances. That's why on top of everything we've already worked on, it's also important to work on determining your guiding principles, connecting to your inner emotional state, and becoming more highly differentiated. Working on knowing your true intentions, and balancing your urge for togetherness and individuality, will allow you to live a more fulfilling life that's aligned with your values, reflects your true choices and desires, and is filled with meaningful and flourishing relationships.

Activity

Are you having trouble connecting with your true intentions, even after writing your belief paper? If so, the questions below will give you a chance to continue uncovering your passions, values, desires, and motivations in a different way. Hopefully, answering them will give you the greatest knowledge you'll ever acquire: a sense of who you are and what you value.

1. What do I love unconditionally?
2. What is my number one accomplishment in life?
3. What do I enjoy doing when no one is watching?
4. If there were no such thing as fear or failure, what would my life look like?
5. If I had $100 million, what would I do?
6. Who is my role model?
7. If I had $30,000 to donate to a cause, which one would I choose?
8. If I went to sleep tonight and a miracle occurred so that all of my problems were gone and I was happy when I woke up, what would be the first thing I'd see? What would my life look like?

These are just a few questions to help you in the process of discovering your true intentions, goals, and values. When you're disconnected from yourself, like Jennifer was, it's hard to know what you want—and it's even harder to make decisions that are right for you. It's natural, when you're overwhelmed by emotions or believe your feelings don't matter to the ones you love, to try numbing and disconnecting from how you truly feel. Instead, try to recognize those emotions, understanding that like a storm, they will pass, and afterwards you'll be able to make decisions and choices for yourself based on your values, principles, and beliefs.

Chapter 10:

MASTER YOUR INNER WORLD

WRITTEN BY ILENE S. COHEN, PH.D.

America will never be destroyed from the outside.
If we falter and lose our freedoms, it will be
because we destroyed ourselves.

– ABRAHAM LINCOLN

SOMETIMES IT FEELS LIKE OUR CULTURE has gone too far in its focus on the pursuit of happiness. There are countless theories in existence about what it means to live a good life. Trust me, I know; I've read up on most of them. Thousands of books, blogs, and websites out there are designed to help us build a happy life, and tons of writers and influencers want to sell us techniques that promise to win us a life of endless bliss. Don't get me wrong, many of these materials provide great wisdom. However, it can all be a bit overwhelming; and some of what's out there makes it easy to believe that it's better to throw in the towel than work on a better life.

In this book, we've tried to present something more than ideas and techniques that will make you happy. Yes, we've offered philosophies, religious perspectives, psychology research outcomes, and activities to help you live a life from *within*. However, our

131

intention isn't to tell you what will make you happy, what will fulfill you, or what you need to do to live your best life. Our hope is that you'll take the information in this book and come up with the answers on your own.

We want this guide to inspire you to function at a higher level and become more aware and intentional with your thoughts and actions. We can't promise you eternal happiness. You'll still have difficult days sometimes, when uncertainty will reign over positivity. The tools we offer here aren't meant to be remedies for all of life's obstacles; rather, they're designed to serve as a road map that can lead you back to yourself, reminding you of your worth, your connection to the world around you, and the fundamental truth that the one thing you're in control of is yourself.

We hope that whenever you find yourself lost, you'll use the ideas we've presented in this book as a reminder to look at the only compass that truly matters, the one built within you from birth: *yourself*. This will help you see what research is starting to validate: that happiness doesn't so much come from pleasure, but rather from a sense of purpose and meaning. No one but you can determine what your purpose is or what will give your life meaning.

When people talk about what makes them happy, it's often some form of hedonic experience —in other words, a two-dimensional sense of joy or pleasure that feels positive in the moment but is inevitably fleeting. Of course, we sometimes search for this pleasure in ways that ultimately make us feel worse, such as by spending impulsively, engaging in irresponsible sexual activities, making unhealthy food choices, or abusing substances. Recent research has been focused on experiences that might not be purely pleasurable in the moment, but that increase our sense of *connectedness* to deeper values. These experiences and connections aren't always easy to forge or figure out, but for most of us, they're our reasons for living. Such experiences often involve a sense of satisfaction with our lives on a deeper level; and, as it turns out, they may just be more valuable than the superficial forms of pleasure many of us mistake for real happiness.

Our overall emotional wellbeing goes deeper than being able to buy that dream car or make more than six figures a year. It comes from cultivating a sense of purpose and having that purpose be an expression of who we are, rather than a way of proving our worth. So, how do we find meaning in a world that offers no shortage of opinions? How do we find lasting satisfaction in a life that can all too easily be filled with sources of immediate, yet short-lived gratification? It seems that many of us are indeed struggling to connect with that deeper sense of meaning. That's why we wrote this book: to get you thinking more deeply about what truly fulfills you, and to support you in finding ways to live from *within*. The way we see it, connecting with a deeper meaning and purpose is always a worthwhile pursuit. But we can only guide you in your quest; the rest of the work is up to you.

When fostering your sense of purpose, here are some important questions to ask yourself:

1. When am I truly in the moment?

2. Whose faces do I see when I think about connection?

3. What am I most willing to put effort into even, if there's no payoff?

4. If I were to write my own obituary, what would be most important to include?

5. If I had a bonus day free from all responsibilities, appointments, and commitments, and I were fully rested, recharged, and able to do anything I wanted for 12 hours, what would I do?

Why It's Important To Do This Work

The Centers for Disease Control and Prevention recently released the shocking statistic that death by suicide is up 25% in the United States from 1999, across most ethnic and age groups. These numbers point to a crisis; however, many are unsure what's creating it. Some argue that this is a crisis of mental health care, as people aren't being provided with the services they need. The traditional solution to this would be providing better-trained therapists, more effective antidepressants, and easier access to treatment. I'm not saying this is misguided; however, the reality is that suicide rates have increased in spite of more people seeking treatment for depression and anxiety, and more treatments for these problems being available than ever before. It seems to me that an additional explanation is needed.

As a practicing therapist, avid reader, and writer, I'm convinced that our nation's suicide crisis is due, in part, to a crisis of meaninglessness. In order to really address this problem, we must understand how cultural shifts in American society, obvious changes in the direction of greater isolation and a decreased sense of belonging, are increasing our risk of existential despair. We have strong instincts to live and survive, to avoid death at all costs. However, our ability to have conscious self-awareness, which has helped us survive in many ways, has also rendered us distinctively reflective. Our ability to contemplate, think about our past and possible future, and wander into deep thought has opened us up to some harsh truths. We understand that we and everyone we care about will likely age, possibly get sick, and certainly die. We know that life is uncertain and unfair at times. We get that pain and sadness are part of our lives. And sometimes, this leads us to wonder: *What's the point of it all?*

In order to keep anxiety about all of our grievances to a minimum, we must understand our purpose and work towards living a meaningful life. We are a species that strives not just for survival, but also for significance. We want our lives to matter. It's when people are unable to maintain a sense of meaning that they're most vulnerable. Studies have shown that people who experience a lack of meaning in their lives are at greater risk of substance abuse, depression, anxiety, and even suicide. People who truly believe that their lives have a purpose are better at dealing with the downfalls of life, including loss, extreme stress, and trauma.

There are many paths to finding a sense of meaning and purpose in life; one of them is laid out in this book. However, it's important to know that close relationships with others are our greatest existential resource. That's why this work is so important: It will help you foster your close relationships and create a real sense of meaning in your life. It's interesting to note that regardless of social class, age, gender, religion, or nationality, people report that the life experiences they find most meaningful typically involve loved ones.

Studies show that it isn't enough to simply be around other people; we need to feel *valued* by them and believe we're making important contributions to a world that matters. This helps explain why we can feel lonely and purposeless, despite being regularly surrounded by people who treat us well. Enjoyable social encounters are not enough to eliminate despair. Compared with earlier generations, we're less likely to know our neighbors, believe that others are trustworthy, or feel we have real connections with people. Studies have shown that the greater their sense of belonging, the more meaningful people consider their lives to be. Other studies have shown that people who feel strongly connected to others perceive life as being more meaningful than lonely people do. Knowing all of this can serve as a necessary catalyst to move our lives in a direction that allows us to feel truly happy and fulfilled—to walk on a path that leads to meaningful happiness, versus the virtually empty kind that comes from instant gratification and living without. The kind that leaves us searching our entire lives for a treasure, all the while using the wrong map.

Daniel, a Case Study

We've provided you with a practical guide to support your search for meaning, true connection, and changing from *within*. Now let's take a look at everything we've presented so far in the form of a case study, so you can see how this process can work in a real-life situation. It's our belief that although it's important to seek new information, we achieve a higher level of learning when we actually apply those ideas to our own lives. Therefore, we want to show you how these ideas look when practically applied, so you can more easily incorporate them in your own situation.

Before he encountered this guide, Daniel was extremely frustrated with himself and his life. He felt like nothing he ever did was good enough, and he found himself continually seeking happiness by working hard for money, getting women's attention, and buying material possessions every time he accomplished a goal at work. Eventually, he found himself at a standstill. He was making the amount of money he always believed would make him happy, he had the affection of beautiful women, and he owned a watch collection that even celebrities would envy. But he still didn't feel happy or content with his life or himself. He was impulsive in his decision-making and found himself aggravated by the smallest things. His lifestyle consisted of overeating and drinking excessively.

Daniel was confused. He'd accomplished everything he thought would make him happy, but he wasn't content at all. All he felt was a constant yearning for more, more, and then some more. That's when he decided to make a change in his life and follow his intuition, which told him that if what he was doing wasn't working, there had to be another way.

Growing up, Daniel knew his family didn't have much money. His parents worked hard, but they lived paycheck to paycheck and weren't always able to provide the basic necessities. They were always comparing prices, clipping coupons, and budgeting. Daniel believed that if his parents had just made more money, he would have had a happier childhood and everyone in the family would have had a better, more peaceful life. He remembered his father getting home from work every day appearing tired and agitated, without much time or energy to spend with his family. Daniel made a promise to himself that when he got older, he'd never struggle like his parents did. He excelled in school, went on to study law, and worked to become partner at a law firm before most people are considered for the title. All of his efforts in life were aimed to ensure that he'd never have to worry about money.

Finally, Daniel reached a point in his life that he didn't really have to worry about money; still, he found himself continuing to strive for more. Whatever he was making, it was never enough. Daniel couldn't understand why making good money and having a successful career weren't ending his discomfort or dissatisfaction. "There must be more to life than work and making money," he thought. "But what?"

Becoming an Observer of Your Own Life

Daniel began the change process by becoming an observer of his life. Instead of acting without thinking, or doing whatever felt good in the moment, he waited and observed himself and his environment. For two weeks, he paid close attention to his body and noticed whatever urges and reactions arose within him; throughout this time, he aimed to observe his life from a more objective standpoint. Daniel was a curious, open-minded journalist exploring a new land. Whenever he felt the need to impulsively react to a situation, he slowed down and asked himself, "What would I like to do in response to this situation?" This allowed him to pause and check in with himself. In doing so, he realized that a lot of his impulsive decisions didn't accurately reflect his values.

Slowing down helped Daniel decide that it was okay to not always be busy working; he didn't have to say yes to every activity his friends and colleagues invited him to, and he didn't need to engage in meaningless encounters with women anymore. Once he got past the initial need to act quickly, he was able to take it easy and relax into better decision-making. Daniel started to understand that his need to go fast and do everything right away derived from his fear of not being successful enough. He was operating from anxiety, which kept him from letting things be as they are. After taking the time to simply observe without acting, Daniel was able to recognize his automatic urge to respond and see that it's okay to go slow sometimes. He wanted to continue this change process by recognizing when he was acting from anxiety instead of from his objective mind.

Our Fundamental Need

Daniel used a scale from 1 to 10—with 1 being the least and 10 being the most—to rate how much of his life was lived from within. He rated himself a 5 and declared that he wanted to work towards being an 8, because he thought his life would feel a lot more fulfilled that way. When living without, Daniel's emotions were always up and down; he never knew what would agitate him from one minute to the next. He didn't feel in control of his life, and he couldn't regulate his feelings. Though he'd try to maintain a good mood, any minor thing that didn't go his way would ruin his entire day. Daniel recognized that if he started to live more from within, his moods wouldn't fluctuate as much, and he'd be able to enjoy a nice day, even if things didn't go his way. Daniel completed the activity in Chapter 2 and came up with the following responses.

1. **Write down the event or interaction that triggered your negative emotion or response.**
   One of my clients didn't like the outcome of his case. He blamed me for being a bad lawyer and demanded his money back.

2. **What emotion or response was triggered in you?**
   I was angry and felt like I didn't do a good job, even though I worked very hard on the case.

3. **Did you consciously decide to have this feeling, or was it an immediate reaction to the event?**
   Those were my automatic thoughts. I took my client's words to mean more than what I knew about myself.

4. **Was your feeling triggered from within or from without?**
   Without.

Through this exercise, Daniel became more aware of how people and circumstances were affecting him. He wasn't trying to fix anything yet; just becoming aware of what was going on in his life was enough to motivate him to make changes. Answering these questions allowed Daniel to reflect and identify an interaction in which something someone said or did triggered a negative emotion or response from him. By writing down the interaction that triggered his negative emotional response, he was able to take a closer look at how much his life was controlled by external circumstances.

The True You

Daniel had a bad habit of telling people what they wanted to hear, instead of being upfront and honest with his thoughts.

This form of people-pleasing was negatively affecting his relation-ships with women and clients at work; people often described him as superficial and fake. At first, it was easy for him to win the affection of others through his charm and flattery. But eventually, people caught on that he wasn't being genuine. Daniel started to make an effort to become more aware of the things he'd think, say, or do to gain acceptance from others. In doing so, he realized that his need to be accepted stemmed from his relationship with his father.

Daniel described his father as hard to please; whenever he'd come home agitated from work, Daniel and his mother would walk on eggshells trying not to upset him. He did whatever he could to make his father proud. Daniel excelled in school and in soccer, because he knew how much these things meant to his father. He couldn't recall ever being authentic or truthful with his father; he made most of his decisions based on what he thought would make his father happy. Starting with this example, he was able to identify many interactions in which he thought, said, or did something to gain someone's acceptance. Below is one example.

- **Write down what you said or did to gain acceptance.**
  When my father asked me about how many goals I scored at a soccer game, I would exaggerate the number. I would lie.

- **What were you hoping to gain from it?**
  I was hoping to gain his love and maintain his acceptance.

Hiding from his true self was a heavy burden for Daniel to carry. He didn't feel close to many people, and casual interactions with others left him feeling drained. It takes a lot of energy to constantly play a role and try to make others happy with you. In fact, most people who go down the road of seeking worthiness from without become completely exhausted by the constant need to satisfy their unquenchable desire for worthiness. When they get burnt out by it, different areas of their lives begin to fall apart. Daniel started noticing that the more he tried to be accepted by people, the more he pushed them away. Becoming aware of how his desire to be accepted began, and seeing how much of what he said was inauthentic, opened his eyes and pushed him to start speaking the truth.

Your Power Space

Daniel started to understand how important it was to simply be aware of why he acted and responded the way he did. For a long time, he'd regularly become reactive—yelling and threatening anyone who upset him—and he had no idea why. Daniel explored the powerful effect of finding the space between stimulus and response using the ***checking into reality*** exercise. Practicing this exercise repeatedly got him into the habit of slowing down his response until he gained more clarity, at which point he could choose a much healthier response. Daniel was particularly sensitive to any form of perceived criticism. Whenever he thought someone was being unappreciative of his hard work, he'd blow up and get defensive. Daniel started to slow down his inner processing system whenever he experienced real or perceived criticism. This gave him the space he needed to choose how he wanted to feel about the situation, instead of falling into an instinctive reaction.

- **Event: Write down the event or interaction that triggered your negative emotion or response.**

  My ex-girlfriend asked me why I didn't hire someone to fix a clog in the sink. She thought I was only capable of being a lawyer, not a handyman.

- **Judgment: Describe your judgment of the event.**
  My ex-girlfriend was critical of my ability to be a real man, the kind who's handy enough to fix things around my house.

- **Feeling: Describe your immediate feeling about the event.**
  Insulted.

- **Space: Describe your feeling after giving yourself some space to reassess the event.**
  After using my space to reassess my judgment, I realize that my judgment may not be true. Additionally, even if my girlfriend at the time thought of me as incapable, I'm still worthy. I'll do my best to honestly decide whether I'm capable or not, while knowing that I'm worthy either way.

- **Response: Describe your response to the event with the perspective you've gained.**
  I might calmly say, "You're right. I'm not great at this, but I enjoy it, so I plan to work on it until I fix it," or, "I'm actually really good at fixing things. I'm sorry you don't think so," or, "You're right. I'm not good at this. Would you mind giving me a hand?" In each case, I'm not becoming a victim of my girlfriend's statement. I'm owning my decision with great responsibility and simply responding to the reality, not any biased feelings I may have about it.

Daniel came to understand that his reactions came from a place of inadequacy and were based in assumptions rather than in the facts of the situation. He would often confuse what he thought of a particular situation with the actual truth. But he came to see that if he didn't slow down, he'd continue to overreact to situations and make unhelpful judgments. By giving himself space to assess one situation at a time, he was free to bring his rational mind into the picture and come up with more helpful responses.

Showing Up

Daniel decided it was best for him to work on speaking truthfully. He'd had trouble establishing meaningful relationships for most of his life, and he figured it was because of his difficulty being honest. He never wanted to be vulnerable. But what he didn't realize was that whenever he was dishonest, even with the small stuff, he was failing to show up authentically. Daniel also had a hard time taking responsibility for his mistakes; instead, he'd become defensive and blame others. He wasn't in touch with his emotions or feelings of inadequacy and would often find himself avoidant, angry, and defensive. But after practicing the ***checking into reality*** exercise, Daniel decided to own his emotions and practice being himself instead of hiding behind his anger. He wanted help to slowly embrace his vulnerabilities and start speaking truthfully, no matter how tough it would be on him.

Daniel took each situation he faced as a challenge to make changes within himself. For example, his mother told him that she didn't like how he'd always show up late to their dinner dates. This got him upset and defensive. He angrily asserted that he was very busy, and that she was lucky he'd made time for her at all. After calming down, he applied the ***checking into reality*** exercise and took responsibility for his fit of anger. He realized that he felt inadequate most of the time, which made him extremely sensitive. Daniel didn't like when people said they were offended by something he did; it was hard for him to take responsibility for his actions. The next time he saw his mother, he apologized for getting upset and thanked her for her honesty. Daniel explained that he reacted the way he did because he personalized her comment instead of realizing how hard it must be for her to always be waiting for him.

To keep the ***checking into reality*** exercise on his mind, Daniel carried around an index card with the following information:

1. **Event:** Write down the event or interaction that triggered your negative emotion or response.

2. **Judgment:** Describe your judgment of the event.

3. **Feeling:** Describe your immediate feeling about the event.

4. **Space:** Describe your feeling after giving yourself some space to reassess the event.

5. **Response:** Describe your response to the event with the perspective you've gained.

Choosing Your Freedom

From a young age, Daniel lived for his father's approval, so he'd never experienced a true sense of freedom, which comes from having the right to live as we believe. This was a foreign concept to Daniel. He felt powerless when facing his father, and as long as he placed his father's needs before his own, he couldn't claim his freedom. Daniel was so busy accommodating the expectations of everyone around him that he forgot to dedicate himself to his own values. But once he started to work on living beginning within, he began to experience liberation. He learned the power of acceptance in himself and his choices, and he stopped basing his personal value on what others thought of him.

It was hard for Daniel to hear his father express disapproval of his choices. Only by accepting the reality in front of him could he take it less personally. Daniel worked on identifying the times when his father frustrated him, so that he could make the choice to accept his father as he is, without judgment. He answered the questions from Chapter 6 as follows.

- **Describe a circumstance or person that normally frustrates you.**

  My father frustrates me when he doesn't accept the choices I make. He's very vocal and demanding when he isn't happy about something. I would usually make decisions to make him happy, because I was scared of his overreactions. It frustrates me that he can't have more reasonable responses. He has to blow up and get angry when he doesn't approve of something.

- **What do you accept about this circumstance or person that frees you from your frustration or judgment?**

  I have learned to not take my father's overreactions personally. It's better to live my life the way I want to, regardless of his opinions, than to live a life that isn't mine. I've realized that my father is just very sensitive and gets mad easily, but that isn't my fault and doesn't mean I'm a bad person. This frees me from frustration and judging myself, accepting my father as he is and accepting myself.

Daniel began to choose freedom, even in his most difficult relationships. It was hard for him to be disapproved of, but it was even more difficult for him to continue trying to seek approval, which led him to constantly live from without, not coming to terms with his own personal truth. As he began to be more open with himself, he was able to see what he truly wants for his life and let go of his fears about what other people think of him.

Your Influential Power

Daniel started to see how capable he was of loving himself and being in relationship with others, without needing to always do and say what they want. He came to understand that we can't reach any depth with others that we haven't reached within ourselves, and that self-acceptance isn't something that happens only when you're perfect. The more he accepted and loved himself, flaws included, the more he was able to accept and love others, even their faults. He worked on *staying focused on others' needs as well as his own, even when they were disapproving or critical of him.* When someone behaved inappropriately, he imagined them drowning in a pool of water. This helped him remain focused on their desperation for worthiness and act immediately to respond to them non-defensively, rather than focusing on his own hurt and taking it personally.

- **Describe the inappropriate or offensive behavior directed towards you.**
  My father was being offensive and disapproving of my actions. He clearly wasn't happy with my recent decision to take one month off from work for travel. I told him that although I appreciate his input, it's my life and my decision to make. But he refused to accept my explanation, became more offensive, and demanded that I take his advice.

- **Envision the person responsible for the behavior drowning from fear of worthlessness.**
  Rather than becoming frustrated by his unwillingness to back off, I recognized that he was drowning in his own fear that I wouldn't listen and would ruin the career I worked so hard to build. I see that he was in no position to back down and understand that it's my life, not his.

- **What's one thing you can do to enhance the other person's sense of worthiness?**
  I reaffirmed that I love him and respect his opinion. I promised him that everything would work out in the end, and that my position as partner wouldn't be jeopardized.

Daniel found a way to respect his father, without necessarily feeling like he needed to give in to his demands. He saw that his father got his sense of worthiness by giving others advice and telling them how to live their lives. Daniel didn't want to see his father drown, but he also wanted the freedom to make his own decisions. So instead of reacting in old ways by taking his father's opinion personally and changing his decisions to appease him, he responded by letting his father know that while he appreciated his input, the decision was his own to make.

The Benefits of Delaying Gratification

Daniel was the king of using temporary forms of instant gratification to ease his discomfort, regardless of the consequences. He desperately wanted to learn how to tolerate the uneasiness he felt whenever he delayed gratification in order to achieve an important goal. It was also important for him to practice resisting his urges to drink excessively and overeat so that he could lose weight and get into good shape. For a long time, Daniel had gained several pounds every year, and he was aware that his health was declining. Still, it was hard for him to resist many of the foods he loved. He was clearly living from without, choosing short-term comforts instead of delaying gratification for a greater goal. But by completing the exercises in this book, Daniel started to get clearer about his goals and the fundamental value of living life with a long-term outlook, instead of seeking short-term gain.

Daniel worked on *moving away from his urge to seek comfort now in order to receive a better reward later.* He continued to identify moments when he really wanted to do something that he knew wouldn't benefit him in the future. In those moments, he called to mind his long-term goals, which helped him to avoid satisfying his desires in the moment. The more he sat with his discomfort, the easier it got for Daniel to resist temptation.

- **Did you sit in your discomfort for a better reward later?**
  I really wanted three drinks after a long day of work. However, one of my goals is to only have one drink twice a week.

- **Did you self-soothe and find the courage to resist immediate gratification?**
  Yes, instead of having an alcoholic beverage, I made chamomile tea and turned on a comedy.

- **Did you get through the urge to feel satisfied now and feel a sense of relief that you didn't give in?**
  I got through the urge to have a drink in order to feel better. I have come to realize that I don't need to drink in order to relax. I still felt relaxed anyway, and I'm losing weight by not drinking as much.

The more Daniel practiced resisting the urge to satisfy his immediate desires, the better he got at dieting, and the more weight he lost. After some practice, he was able to apply this to many other aspects of his life. For example, he was previously impulsive when it came to dating and felt the need to line up several dates, even if he wasn't too interested in the person he was taking out. Instead of seeking the comfort of always having a date planed, he waited to make plans with women he thought he could actually connect with long-term. It was difficult at first; but over time, Daniel started to feel better about his actions aligning with his long-term goals. He was beginning to see his life unfold in the ways he'd always wanted it to, simply by resisting his impulses. He lost weight and started exclusively dating someone he met through friends. It became important for Daniel to be healthy, maintain his successful performance at work, make time for himself, and start a family with someone. His life was no longer just about making money and staying busy. He'd always wanted more for himself, but it wasn't until he slowed down and took a closer look at himself that this vision started to materialize.

Living Intentionally

This book helped Daniel on his quest to live more intentionally. For as long as he could remember, he'd been on autopilot, reacting to his circumstances instead of making decisions based on his long-term goals and values. He was discontent and never satisfied, unaware of why he wasn't happy. He learned that if he wanted to live from within, he couldn't keep making decisions based on reactions to his outside circumstances. Daniel worked hard to determine his guiding principles, connect to his inner emotional state, and become more highly differentiated. Working on knowing his true intentions allowed him to live a more fulfilling life that aligned with his values. His health, relationships, and life improved in many ways. He no longer felt like his life was out of his control. He didn't feel the need to always be busy, or to tell people what they wanted to hear.

Daniel wrote a list of his beliefs that he referred back to whenever he felt lost or impulsive. By having a purpose and making decisions more intentionally, he finally took ownership of his life. Feeling healthy, knowing he was worthy, having the ability to manage his emotions, and enjoying his close personal relationships were more fulfilling to him than making more money.

The big takeaway from Daniel's story is that sometimes we think we know what will make us happy and feel fulfilled, but we're mistaken. Daniel was so sure his parents' unhappiness would be relieved if only he'd make more money; but in reality, that would never have been the case. Daniel was able to accomplish goals and live the life he'd dreamed about as a child; what a surprise it was to him when he still didn't feel so great about his life. By slowing down, becoming more aware, looking within, and responding versus reacting to life, he was able to connect to his true intentions, as well as to the people around him.

Conclusion

Whatever your faith or beliefs may be, it's impossible to deny that we're all connected in some way. We all seek worthiness, meaning, and love. We all want to know that we matter, that our lives have a purpose. This notion lies deeply within the consciousness of every human being. Knowing what you're going to do with your time on earth, and believing wholeheartedly in your inherent worthiness, is invaluable. Of course, you can continue to chase external rewards, live on autopilot, and eat junk all you want; it's your life, after all. But we hope that whatever life you design for yourself, you'll do it deliberately and intentionally. We hope that you'll live knowing that you're worthy of whatever you choose.

Daniel could have continued on the path of working, eating, drinking, and sleeping; no one would have said he had it very bad. However, he wasn't choosing his life; he was just floating through it. We all have the option to coast through life and blame our inconveniences and disappointments on external circumstances. However, we can also take life more seriously, taking initiative and taking responsibility for ourselves. It might not be the easier path at first, but it's the only one that leads to anywhere worthwhile. It's the only way to master our inner world.

Whether it's society's pressure, our culture, or the drive to try and make everyone happy around us, we all face obstacles to going deeper within our reality. This can leave us feeling unfulfilled, anxious, and depressed, searching for meaning outside of ourselves, and trying anything to develop a real connection. Many of us feel that money or fame will fulfill us. We believe the story sold to us that building a company, finding a perfect partner, having a great career, or traveling the world will lead us to true happiness. We search all over for that peaceful sense of fulfillment, and we struggle to find it. Because it's not outside ourselves; it's within us.

BIBLIOGRAPHY

BAER, G. (2004). *Real Love: The Truth About Finding Unconditional Love & Fulfilling Relationships.* Penguin Random House, New York.

BEAUGARD, M. and O'LEARY, D. (2008). *The Spiritual Brain: A Neuroscientist's Case for the Existence of the Soul.* HarperCollins, New York.

BOWEN, M. (1978). *Family Therapy in Clinical Practice.* Jason Aronson, New York.

BROWN, J. (2012). *Growing Yourself Up: How to Bring Your Best to All of Life's Relationships.* Exisle, New Zealand.

FRANKL, V.E. (1959). *Man's Search for Meaning.* Beacon Press, Massachusetts.

FREEMAN, T. (2012). *Bringing Heaven Down to Earth.* Vol 11.

KERR, M.E. and BOWEN, M. (1988). *Family Evaluation: An Approach Based on Bowen Theory.* Norton, New York.

NOONE, R.J. and PAPERO, D.V. (2015). *The Family Emotional System: An Integrative Concept for Theory, Science, and Practice.* Lexington Books, Maryland.

SCHIRALDI, G.R. (2016). *The Self-Esteem Workbook.* New Harbinger Publications, Inc., Oakland, CA.

SCHWARTZ, J.M. and BEGLEY, S. (2003). *The Mind & The Brain: Neuroplasticity and the Power of Mental Force.* Regan Books, New York.

TITELMAN, P. (Ed.) (2008). *Triangles: Bowen Family Systems Theory Perspectives.* Haworth Clinical Practice Press, New York.
Likkutei Torah, Parshat Shelach Tzava'at Harivash 10

ACKNOWLEDGMENTS

From Rabbi Aryeh Weinstein

To Rosie, my wife, my rock, and my guide. Your wisdom and acceptance have made me anew. All the insights, and all the time taken to make this book, are thanks to you.

To my beloved parents, Rabbi Naftoli and Sherry Weinstein, for bringing me to this world, giving me a Jewish education, and raising me with the values that have given me everything I now teach and share. To my father-in-law, Rabbi Yehoshua, and mother-in-law, Sara Balkany, for all your love and support, and for raising and guiding the girl who has become my wife.

A special thank you to Rabbi Yudy Shemtov, Executive Director and Senior Rabbi of Lubavitch of Bucks County, for your continuous support, and for providing the platform supporting all of my work.

Thank you to Brandon and Lisa Swartz, and Neil and Hedy Hoffman, for your sincere friendship and support, and for always believing in me. To my community, thank you for trusting me, supporting me, and sharing your lives with me.

To Rabbi Dr. Laibl Wolf, Rabbi Simon Jacobson and Michael and Estelle Rabinowitz, thank you for taking the time to review the manuscript and offer many helpful suggestions.

To our editor, Dr. Denise Fournier, thank you for your hard work in turning our transcripts into a real book.

From Dr. Ilene Cohen

I would like to acknowledge many people who contributed to the completion of this book:

To my subscribers and loyal audience, who give me the motivation to do the work I do, thank you for your continuous support and input. Without you, this book would not have been possible.

To my clients, whose contribution to this book I could never overstate, thank you for opening up to me and letting me share your stories so that others can learn from your experiences and enhance their own lives.

To the careful readers who made many helpful suggestions, including Jasmine Terrany, Dr. Edrica Richardson, Corinne Debacher, Dr. Oliva S. Colmer, Dr. Jim Rudes, Michelle Dempsey, and Donna Strauss, I offer my sincerest gratitude.

To our wonderful editor, Dr. Denise Fournier, thank you for all of your hard work and edits. You transformed our book into a beautiful piece of work.

A warm thank you to my family, whom I love more than anything, Moises, Emily, Elizabeth, Lea, Alberto and Abe Cohen, Donna, Michael, Molly, Matthew, Michelle and Danielle Strauss.

And a final but deep thank you to all my readers, who have opened their minds and hearts to make real and genuine changes in their lives.

INDEX

W
WWII, 16-17
worthiness
    experiencing, 25
    from within, xviii, xxii, 13, 18,
        51, 70
    from without, xviii, xxii, 13-14, 18
    inherent, xviii, 23-24, 47-48,
        55, 86, 150
    lack of, xxi
    need for, 50, 88, 93
    seeking, xviii, xxiii, 38, 140,
        146, 150
    sense of, xix, xxiv, 9, 13, 15, 26,
        30, 59, 146-147

Y
yetzer hara, 54

Z
Zushe, Reb, 46

About the Authors

Rabbi Aryeh Weinstein

Rabbi Aryeh Weinstein is a dedicated father, raising nine children with his wife, Rosie. He is the director of the Jay Michael Swartz Jewish Learning Academy, and his engaging teaching style has made him a critically acclaimed and sought-after speaker and podcaster. His courses, which offer a blend of psychology, spirituality, clarity, and conviction, are used by hundreds of Rabbis in preparation for their own courses. His unique method teaches people to start living life from within, rather than allowing people and circumstances to define their emotional state.

Ilene S. Cohen

"Dr. Ilene" S. Cohen, Ph.D. is a psychotherapist, professor, blogger and author of the popular self-help guide, *When It's Never About You*. Her work regularly appears in top psychology publications.

After graduating from the University of Tampa with a B.A. in Psychology, Dr. Ilene obtained her Master's and Ph.D. degrees in Marriage and Family Therapy from Nova Southeastern University. Both her books and her practice are fueled by her passion for helping people achieve their goals, build a strong sense of self, and lead meaningful lives. She is also guided by a passion for service and lends her time to multiple charitable causes around the world. Dr. Ilene resides in Miami, Florida with her husband and two young daughters.

Made in the USA
Las Vegas, NV
29 March 2021

20368407R00107